impact

1A

SERIES EDITORS
JoAnn (Jodi) Crandall
Joan Kang Shin

STUDENT'S BOOK AUTHOR
Lesley Koustaff

NATIONAL GEOGRAPHIC
LEARNING

Australia · Brazil · Mexico · Singapore · United Kingdom · United States

Thank you to the educators who provided invaluable feedback during the development of *Impact*:

EXPERT PANEL

Márcia Ferreira, Academic Coordinator, CCBEU, Franca, Brazil

Jianwei Song, Vice-general Manager, Ensure International Education, Harbin, China

María Eugenia Flores, Academic Director, and **Liana Rojas-Binda**, Head of Recruitment & Training, Centro Cultural Costarricense-Norteamericano, San José, Costa Rica

Liani Setiawati, M.Pd., SMPK 1 BPK PENABUR Bandung, Bandung, Indonesia

Micaela Fernandes, Head of Research and Development Committee and Assessment Committee, Pui Ching Middle School, Macau

Héctor Sánchez Lozano, Academic Director, and **Carolina Tripodi**, Head of the Juniors Program, Proulex, Guadalajara, Mexico

Rosario Giraldez, Academic Director, Alianza Cultural, Montevideo, Uruguay

REVIEWERS

BRAZIL

Renata Cardoso, Colégio do Sol, Guara, DF

Fábio Delano Vidal Carneiro, Colégio Sete de Setembro, Fortaleza

Cristiano Carvalho, Centro Educacional Leonardo da Vinci, Vitória

Silvia Corrêa, Associação Alumni, São Paulo

Carol Espinosa, Associação Cultural Brasil Estados Unidos, Salvador

Marcia Ferreira, Centro Cultural Brasil Estados Unidos, Franca

Clara Haddad, ELT Consultant, São Paulo

Elaine Carvalho Chaves Hodgson, Colégio Militar de Brasília, Brasília

Thays Farias Galvão Ladosky, Associação Brasil América, Recife

Itana Lins, Colégio Anchieta, Salvador

Samantha Mascarenhas, Associação Cultural Brasil Estados Unidos, Salvador

Ann Marie Moreira, Pan American School of Bahia, Bahia

Rodrigo Ramirez, CEETEPS- Fatec Zona Sul, São Paulo

Paulo Torres, Vitória Municipality, Vitória

Renata Zainotte, Go Up Idiomas, Rio de Janeiro

CHINA

Zhou Chao, MaxEn Education, Beijing

Zhu Haojun, Only International Education, Shanghai

Su Jing, Beijing Chengxun International English School, Beijing

Jianjun Shen, Phoenix City International School, Guangzhou

COSTA RICA

Luis Antonio Quesada-Umaña, Centro Cultural Costarricense Norteamericano, San José

INDONESIA

Luz S. Ismail, M.A., LIA Institute of Language and Vocational Training, Jakarta

Selestin Zainuddin, LIA Institute of Language and Vocational Training, Jakarta

Rosalia Dian Devitasari, SMP Kolese Kanisius, Jakarta

JAPAN

John Williams, Tezukayama Gakuen, Nara

MEXICO

Nefertiti González, Instituto Mexicano Madero, Puebla

Eugenia Islas, Instituto Tlalpan, Mexico City

Marta MM Seguí, Colegio Velmont A.C., Puebla

SOUTH KOREA

Min Yuol (Alvin) Cho, Global Leader English Education, Yong In

THAILAND

Panitnan Kalayanapong, Eduzone Co., Ltd., Bangkok

TURKEY

Damla Çaltuğ, İELEV, Istanbul

Basak Nalcakar Demiralp, Ankara Sinav College, Ankara

Humeyra Olcayli, İstanbul Bilim College, Istanbul

VIETNAM

Chantal Kruger, ILA Vietnam, Hô Chí Minh

Ai Nguyen Huynh, Vietnam USA Society, Hô Chí Minh

impact

1A

	1 Life in the City *page 8*	**2** Amazing Jobs *page 24*	**3** Secrets of the Dark *page 42*	**4** Living Together *page 58*
THEME	Exploring your city or town	Unusual and interesting careers	The world at night	Animal and human interaction
VOCABULARY STRATEGIES	· Prefix *un-* · Use context	· Suffixes *-er*, *-or* and *-ist* · Identify word parts (suffixes)	· Compound words · Use a dictionary: Most common meaning	· Prefix *mis-* · Identify collocations
SPEAKING STRATEGY	Active listening	Extending the conversation	Asking for help and helping with schoolwork	Asking for and giving reasons
GRAMMAR	**Present simple:** Talking about facts *I live near the High Line.* **In and on:** Expressing location *Lion City is in eastern China.*	**Present simple questions and answers:** Talking about routines *Do pastry chefs work every day? Yes, they do. / No, they don't.* **Possessives:** Showing ownership *This dentist's job isn't done in an office.*	**Present continuous:** Saying what is happening now *While I'm reading in bed at night in Mexico, my friend Akiko is reading at school in Japan!* **At, on and in:** Saying when things happen *at eight o'clock, on Monday(s), in the winter*	**Modals:** Describing obligation and advice *We have to protect rhinos. We shouldn't ignore the rhino problem.* **Modals:** Describing ability in the present and the past *What can we do about it? How could they avoid cars?*
READING	*A New Type of Park*	*Adventures Near and Far*	*In the Dark of the Ocean*	*Four-legged heroes*
READING STRATEGY	Make predictions	Compare and contrast	Scan the text	Identify problems and solutions
VIDEO	*Mission Re-Wild*	*Searching for Life in Iceland's Fissures*	*What Glows Beneath*	*The Elephant Whisperers*
WRITING	Genre: **Descriptive paragraph** Focus: Use adjectives	Genre: **Descriptive paragraph** Focus: Identify and include elements of a paragraph	Genre: **Descriptive paragraph** Focus: Use sensory writing	Genre: **Descriptive paragraph** Focus: Proofread
MISSION	**Explore Your World** National Geographic Explorer: **Daniel Raven-Ellison**, Guerilla Geographer	**Do What You Love** National Geographic Explorer: **Guillermo de Anda**, Underwater Archaeologist	**Understand and Protect** National Geographic Explorer: **David Gruber**, Marine Biologist	**Start Small** National Geographic Explorer: **Amy Dickman**, Animal Conservationist
PRONUNCIATION	Syllables and stress	Intonation in questions	Present continuous: Stress of the verb *be*	*Can* and *can't*
EXPRESS YOURSELF	Creative Expression: **Travel review** *Gondola Tours of Venice* Making connections: Unusual places and unusual jobs		Creative Expression: **Graphic story** *Sleeping with a Lion* Making connections: Interactions between humans and animals at night	

Unit 1

DANIEL RAVEN-ELLISON **Guerrilla Geographer**

Daniel Raven-Ellison believes that guerrilla geography helps you to see the world around you in new ways. Daniel explores urban areas. He has walked across many cities, taking a picture after every eight steps! Daniel wants everyone to get outdoors, explore and discover the surprises that the world has for us.

Unit 2

GUILLERMO DE ANDA **Underwater Archaeologist**

Guillermo de Anda explores caves in the Yucatán Peninsula in Mexico, sometimes for more than 12 hours at a time. He's searching for artefacts from the Mayan civilization. When he explores, Guillermo faces challenges like swimming in small spaces and dodging swarms of bats. Would you enjoy this unusual job?

Unit 3

DAVID GRUBER **Marine Biologist**

David Gruber has always loved the sea. When he was a teenager, he learnt to surf. While he surfed, he wondered what was below the waves. Now David is a marine biologist. He studies underwater animals that make their own light. David wants to understand these incredible creatures and why they glow.

Unit 4

AMY DICKMAN **Animal Conservationist**

When Amy Dickman was young, she wanted to work with big cats. Today, as an animal conservationist, she does just that! Amy works in Tanzania giving talks, meeting local villagers and helping people understand how to live with and help big cats. Amy thinks small actions, such as talking to others about endangered animals, can make a big difference.

Life in the City

'Geography is about curiosity, exploration and discovery. It gives you the power to see places in new ways, search for your own answers and make sense of the world.'

Daniel Raven-Ellison

A red fox exploring Bristol, UK

TO START

1. Look at the photo. If you saw this in person, would it surprise you? Why or why not?

2. The animal in the photo is exploring. Do you explore? Why is it good to explore a new place?

3. What is your favourite place? What do you do there? Why is this place special to you?

9

1 **What makes Astana different from other cities?** Discuss. Then listen and read. ∩ **002**

The city of Astana is truly a **unique** place. It was **constructed** in 1997 to replace the city of Almaty as the **capital** of Kazakhstan. Almaty was in the south-eastern corner of the country, but the president of Kazakhstan wanted a new capital. So Astana was built right in the middle of the country. As a result, this modern city is **surrounded by** nothing but rural areas.

The unusual **architecture** of Astana makes it look like a space-age city. There are amazing **skyscrapers** and eye-catching buildings. A cultural centre looks like a big, blue eye. A university building has the **shape** of a dog bowl.

The Bayterek Tower in central Astana

Another unusual building, the Bayterek **Tower**, is a **symbol** of the city. This tall structure is 105 m. (345 ft.) high and looks like an enormous tree with a golden egg inside.

A Japanese architect named Kisho Kurokawa won first prize in a competition to **design** and **plan** the new capital. He included many parks and public spaces to connect urban life with nature.

Astana has pleasant summers. But the weather can get very cold in the winter, with temperatures dropping to -40°C (-40°F). Because of its extreme climate, Astana offers a lot of **indoor** entertainment. A popular entertainment centre is the Khan Shatyr, or king's tent, the world's largest tent. Inside, there is a river for boating, a park, an indoor running track, a waterslide and even a sandy beach with palm trees! The **residents** of Astana can enjoy a variety of outdoor activities even when it's well below freezing.

The Khan Shatyr

2 **LEARN NEW WORDS Listen and repeat.** ⌂ 003

3 **Work in pairs.** Compare Astana to the place where you live. What do you like and dislike about each place? Would you like to live in Astana? Why or why not?

4 **Read and write the words from the list.** Make any necessary changes.

architecture	capital	outdoors	plan
resident	skyscraper	surrounded by	unique

Daniel Raven-Ellison has a very _____ job: he's a guerrilla geographer. He loves exploring places and making discoveries. Daniel says that we are _____ interesting things just waiting to be discovered. According to him, _____ of a place should keep exploring. They can make new discoveries even if they've lived in the same place their whole lives. Daniel _____ all kinds of exciting adventures. In one adventure, he climbed more than 3,300 floors of the many tall _____ in London. In another, he walked across Mexico City, the _____ of Mexico. He photographed everything he saw in front of him every eight steps. He took photos of _____ , streets and public spaces. He's done the same thing in 12 other cities!

5 **LEARN NEW WORDS Listen to these words and match them with the definitions.** Then listen and repeat. 🎧 004 005

rural	unusual	urban

_____ 1. different or uncommon

_____ 2. relating to the countryside

_____ 3. relating to the city

Daniel Raven-Ellison

6 **YOU DECIDE Choose an activity.**

1. **Work independently.** Go on a discovery walk outdoors. Find things that are hard, soft, sticky, brown, pink, small, big or smelly. Take photos and present your experience to the class.

2. **Work in pairs.** Think of two adventures you can have near your home. Why would you choose these adventures? What can you learn from them?

3. **Work independently.** Walk through your school building and take photographs every eight steps. What interesting things do you see? Create a photo book of your discoveries.

SPEAKING STRATEGY 🎧 006

Active listening

Really?	You're kidding!
Wow!	Seriously?
No way!	That's <u>incredible</u>!

1 **Listen.** How do the speakers show they're listening actively? Write the words and phrases you hear. 🎧 007

2 **Read and complete the dialogue.**

Dad: Meiling, look at this. I found this old map of our city. It's more than 100 years old.

Meiling: _____ Let me see.

Dad: This building was a hospital. It's a music hall now.

Meiling: _____

Dad: I know! And this was the old library.

Meiling: _____ Now it's a tall skyscraper.

Dad: And look. This was a park.

Meiling: _____ It's my school now!

Dad: Hey, let's go for a walk. We can take the map and look for other changes.

Meiling: Great idea! I'll bring my camera and take some photos.

3 **Work in groups.** Take turns. Choose a card. Read the question and the possible answers. Group members guess the correct answer and use active listening to respond to the real answer.

One million?
That's amazing!

How many ants are there for every person in the world?

A. one thousand
B. one million
C. six million

B. one million

Go to page 153.

4 **Work in pairs.** Think of an interesting place, thing or event in your neighbourhood, and describe it to your partner. Your partner should use the words and phrases above to show active listening. When you finish, swap roles.

Present simple: Talking about facts

I **live** near the High Line.

She **works** next to the High Line.

Cars **don't drive** on the High Line.

You **go** to concerts on the High Line.

The High Line **doesn't allow** pets.

We **walk** through the High Line's gardens.

1 **Listen.** You will hear eight facts about the High Line. For each fact, circle the present simple form you hear. 🎧 009

1.	grow	grows	don't grow	5.	need	needs	don't need
2.	visit	visits	doesn't visit	6.	enjoy	enjoys	don't enjoy
3.	open	opens	doesn't open	7.	sell	sells	doesn't sell
4.	close	closes	doesn't close	8.	get	gets	don't get

2 **Read.** Complete the sentences with the correct present simple form of the verbs in brackets.

1. The High Line _____ open all night. (not stay)

2. The High Line _____ special chairs for relaxing. (have)

3. A tour guide _____ about the High Line's gardens. (talk)

4. Musicians _____ concerts on Saturday afternoons. (give)

5. Visitors _____ to walk along the High Line. (not pay)

3 **Work in pairs.** Take turns saying facts about the High Line. Use the present simple.

1. the High Line / have / a play area for children
2. you / not / need / a ticket for the High Line
3. many different animals / live / on the High Line
4. guides / give / free tours to visitors
5. he / attend / exercise classes on the High Line
6. I / want / to visit the High Line

The High Line in
New York City, USA

LEARN NEW WORDS Read about the Cheonggyecheon Stream park in Seoul, Korea. Then listen and repeat. 🎧 010 011

Cheonggyecheon Stream

In 2003, the mayor of Seoul decided to remove a **motorway** over an underground **stream**. He wanted the area around the stream to be an urban green space for people to enjoy. Today, the six-kilometre (four-mile) park on either side of the Cheonggyecheon Stream provides a place for people to relax.

At the park, visitors attend traditional festivals and concerts. They enjoy cultural events, look at art, and watch water and light shows. Many people just walk along the **pavements** or over one of 22 **bridges**, each with its own design and meaning.

5 **Read and complete the sentences.** Make any necessary changes.

bridge	motorway	pavement	stream

1. The Cheonggyecheon Stream was covered by a _____ .

2. Now visitors go for walks on the _____ near the water.

3. People enjoy water shows over the _____ .

4. Each of the _____ has a unique look and meaning.

6 **Work in groups.** Name an interesting outdoor place where you live. How do people enjoy this place? What can you see and do at this place? Use the present simple.

1 **BEFORE YOU READ Discuss in pairs.** Look at the title and the photo. What do you think the reading is about?

2 **LEARN NEW WORDS Look at the words below.** What do you think they mean?

concrete	land	outdoor	park

Now find them in the reading. Has your idea about the meaning changed? Explain. Then listen and repeat. 🎧 012

3 **WHILE YOU READ Look for words and phrases that support your prediction.** 🎧 013

4 **AFTER YOU READ Look at the sentences.** Tick T for *true* or F for *false*.

1. London is now a national park city. (T) (F)

2. London has 13,000 parks. (T) (F)

3. London has a lot of green spaces. (T) (F)

4. Most children in London spend their days playing outside. (T) (F)

5. Daniel wants people to spend more time outdoors. (T) (F)

A New Type of Park

Can the capital of England become a national park?

Imagine stepping out of your front door and standing in the middle of a national park. Daniel Raven-Ellison hopes this might soon be possible for millions of London residents. Daniel is leading a campaign to make London a national park city.

Although London has much more concrete than a national park usually would, it is home to more than 13,000 kinds of wildlife. These species live in its 3,000 parks, along with 1,500 varieties of flowering plants and more than 300 species of birds. In fact, 47 per cent of the land in London is green space.

'We have eight million trees in London; it's the world's largest urban forest,' Daniel says. That's almost one tree for every person living in London! Yet, even though London has thousands of outdoor spaces, one in seven children living there hasn't visited a green space in the past year.

Daniel believes that making London into a national park will protect the animal life and green spaces in London. He hopes it will also encourage people, especially young people, to spend more time outdoors. Daniel takes his own son out to explore in London, and he thinks that other parents should do the same. Daniel is convinced that people who spend a lot of time in nature live happier and healthier lives. What do you think?

5 **Check your predictions.** Look at your predictions from Activity 1. Were you correct? What surprised you in this reading?

6 **Discuss in groups.**

1. How often do you visit green spaces? In your opinion, is it enough? What things do you do there?

2. Do you think that turning your city into a national park would be good? Why or why not?

3. Imagine that you can make changes in your city. Which places do you want to protect? Which places do you want to change? How do you want to change them? Explain your answers.

1. Seoul, Korea   2.3%

2. Hong Kong, China   2.5%

3. Mumbai, India   4.4%

4. Bogotá, Colombia   41%

5. Moscow, Russia   47%

6. Singapore   54%

② **Read and circle.** You're going to watch *Mission Re-Wild*. From the title and the photo, predict what the video is about. Circle the letter.

a. Putting wild animals back into forests

b. Building more skyscrapers in cities

c. Making more green space in cities

③ WHILE YOU WATCH **Check your guesses from Activity 1.** How many were correct? Watch scene 1.1.

A mural made from moss by artist Carly Schmitt

4 **AFTER YOU WATCH Read the sentences.** Circle the correct answer.

1. Cities with *a lot of* / *very little* green space are sometimes called *concrete jungles*.

2. Seoul and Mumbai have *a lot of* / *very little* green space.

3. People who spend time outdoors are *happier* / *unhappier* than people who don't.

4. You can enjoy the outdoors *in both rural and urban areas* / *only in rural areas*.

5. *Only some cities have* / *Every city has* signs of natural life.

6. One way to start re-wilding is *planting a tree* / *recycling plastic*.

5 **Work in pairs.** Put the steps for re-wilding a city in the correct order.

_____ Birds build nests in the tree.

__1__ Plant a seed in the ground.

_____ People like seeing the tree and the birds.

_____ The seed grows into a small tree.

_____ Other people begin to plant trees, too.

6 **Discuss in pairs.**

1. How much public green space is there where you live? Would you like more? Why or why not?

2. Why do you think some places have more public green space than other places?

7 **YOU DECIDE Choose an activity.**

1. **Work independently.** Imagine you're going to re-wild a space where you live. Where is it? How will you do it? Make a plan and present it to the class.

2. **Work in pairs.** Find out about a place that was successfully re-wilded. How did it change? How do people enjoy it now? Write a paragraph and use photos to explain what you learnt.

3. **Work in groups.** Prepare a 'Let's Re-Wild' poster to teach others about re-wilding. Write three reasons why it is good to re-wild. Write ideas on what people can do. Draw pictures of a space before and after it has been re-wilded.

In and *on*: Expressing location

Lion City is **in** eastern China.

There are many beautiful bridges **in** Lion City.

Lion City is **in** the water.

China is **on** the continent of Asia.

Lion City is one of the most unique places **on** Earth.

Lion City is not **on** a mountain.

1 **Listen.** Write *in* or *on* in the spaces below. 015

1. There are many ancient cities _____ Asia, such as Shi Cheng, also known as Lion City.

2. Shi Cheng is an ancient city located _____ China.

3. Visitors to Shi Cheng today can't walk _____ its streets to admire it.

4. It isn't _____ a mountain or _____ an island. It's _____ the water!

5. _____ Shi Cheng, there are 265 archways crossing over its streets.

6. There are beautiful sculptures of lions, dragons and birds _____ these archways.

2 **Work in pairs.** Listen to the passage again. Write two additional facts about Shi Cheng. Use *on* and *in* in your sentences. 016

_____

_____

3 **Work in groups.** Take turns using the spinner. Make sentences using *in* or *on*.

About seven billion people live on Earth.

Go to page 155.

In descriptive writing, we try to create a picture for the reader. We use describing words to help the reader clearly imagine what we're writing about. Examples of describing words include:

beautiful   **colourful**   **new**   **short**   **sweet-smelling**   **yellow**

1 **Read the model.** Work in pairs to find and underline all of the describing words the writer uses to talk about the garden.

    Last year, the empty space opposite my bus stop was a sad, empty, ugly space, with only a couple of dead bushes and one short tree. Then some hard-working gardeners in the neighbourhood changed that. They were tired of looking at that sad space while waiting for the bus, so they made it into a beautiful garden. Now, on a sunny summer day you can look across the street and see colourful vegetable plants and sweet-smelling flowers while you wait for the bus. Yellow butterflies fly from plant to plant, and tiny birds sing in the green trees. I love taking the bus now!

2 **Work in pairs.** Draw a picture of the garden described in Activity 1. Compare your drawing with a partner's. How are they the same? How are they different?

3 **Write.** Think of a beautiful place in your neighbourhood. Use describing words to write a paragraph about this place.

Explore Your World

'There are amazing adventures to be had right outside our doors.'

Daniel Raven-Ellison

National Geographic Explorer, Guerrilla Geographer

1. Watch scene 1.2.

2. Daniel thinks it's best for students to experience geography rather than just read about it. What other school subjects can you explore outside the classroom? How can you explore them?

3. How much of your town or city have you explored? What else is there to learn about where you live? Keep a journal of outdoor adventures you have in your area.

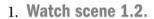

Make an Impact

YOU DECIDE Choose a project.

1 **Conduct a survey.**

· Ask your friends how much time they spent indoors and outdoors in the past week.

· Calculate the average amount of indoor and outdoor time.

· Present your findings to the class. Give suggestions for spending more time outdoors.

2 **Plan and conduct a scavenger hunt.**

· Work as a group to prepare a list of items to find in a local green space.

· Work independently to find the items on the list.

· Discuss which items on the list were the easiest and the most difficult to find.

3 **Write a newspaper article.**

· Think of someone who has lived in your neighbourhood for a long time. Write questions to ask them about your neighbourhood.

· Interview that person. Find maps and photos to show the changes that he or she describes.

· Write a newspaper article to summarise the interview and show the changes.

Amazing Jobs

NASA astronauts working underwater on a
Hubble space telescope model

'We're always in search of something. My job is a combination of extreme sports, nature, mystery, science and reading.'
Guillermo de Anda

TO START

1. What do you think the people in this photo are doing? Does it look easy or difficult? Explain.

2. Which jobs involve a lot of physical activity or danger? Why do you think people do these jobs?

3. Would you enjoy a job that combines nature, science and extreme sports? Why or why not?

What do underwater **adventure**, detective work and Mayan history have in common? They're all part of the unusual **profession** of Guillermo de Anda. He's a college professor and an underwater **archaeologist**. Guillermo's **job** is to **explore** flooded underground areas known as *cenotes*. 'It's unusual **work** for a lot of people,' Guillermo says about his job. 'It's hard, but it's a lot of fun as well.'

Guillermo dives to learn more about Mayan culture. About 2,000 years ago, the Maya lived in the Yucatán Peninsula of Mexico, the area Guillermo explores. Guillermo dives there now to look for ancient Mayan artefacts underwater. He **studies** them for **clues** about how the Maya lived.

The inside of a cenote

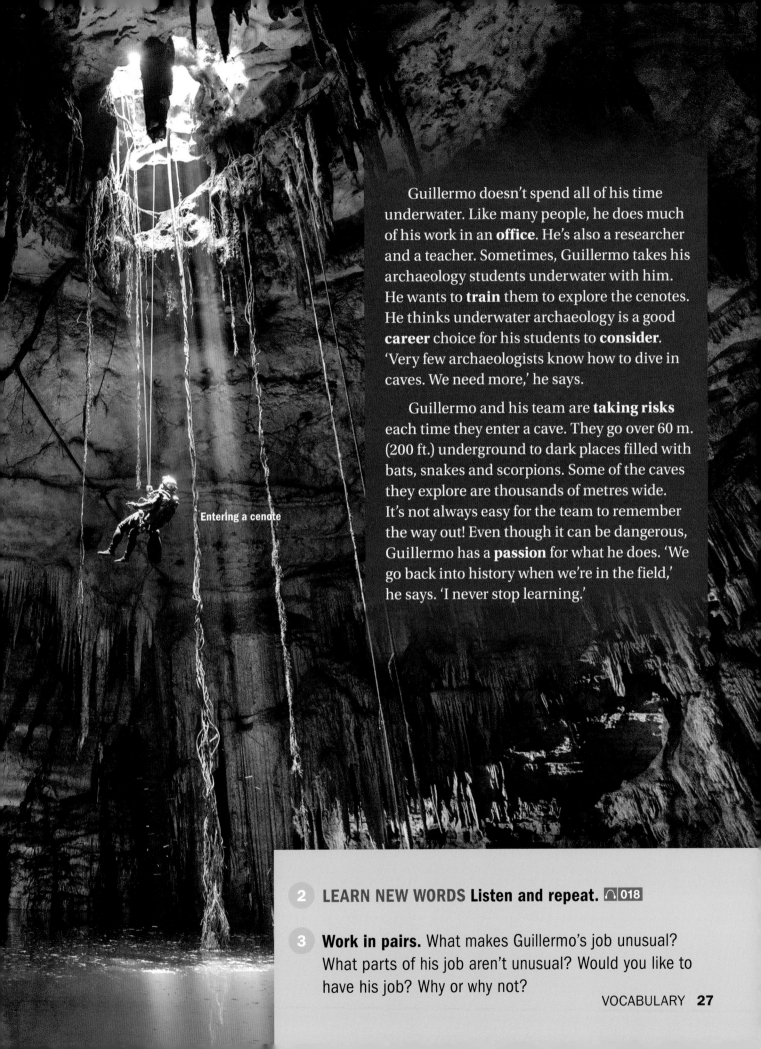

Entering a cenote

Guillermo doesn't spend all of his time underwater. Like many people, he does much of his work in an **office**. He's also a researcher and a teacher. Sometimes, Guillermo takes his archaeology students underwater with him. He wants to **train** them to explore the cenotes. He thinks underwater archaeology is a good **career** choice for his students to **consider**. 'Very few archaeologists know how to dive in caves. We need more,' he says.

Guillermo and his team are **taking risks** each time they enter a cave. They go over 60 m. (200 ft.) underground to dark places filled with bats, snakes and scorpions. Some of the caves they explore are thousands of metres wide. It's not always easy for the team to remember the way out! Even though it can be dangerous, Guillermo has a **passion** for what he does. 'We go back into history when we're in the field,' he says. 'I never stop learning.'

2 **LEARN NEW WORDS Listen and repeat.** 🎧 018

3 **Work in pairs.** What makes Guillermo's job unusual? What parts of his job aren't unusual? Would you like to have his job? Why or why not?

4 Read and circle the correct word.

Do you like *adventure / profession*? Do you want a job that isn't in *a clue / an office*? Do you want to *consider / explore* underwater but don't know how to dive? If you answered *yes*, then you might like *a career / an archaeologist* as a Remotely Operated Vehicle (ROV) operator.

ROV operators help underwater *archaeologists / offices* like Guillermo de Anda. ROV operators help look for *professions / clues* about old objects and the people who used them. Explorers like Guillermo also use ROVs to decide what parts of a cave they should explore. Divers *don't study / take risks* when they dive into caves, so ROV operators can help them make choices about where to explore. If your *passion / career* is exploring, consider becoming an ROV operator.

5 LEARN NEW WORDS Listen and complete the sentences with the correct word. Then listen and repeat. 🎧 019 020

choice	dangerous	researcher

1. If a job is _____ , it isn't safe.

2. When you make a _____ , you decide what you want.

3. A _____ studies people or objects to learn more about them.

An ROV

6 YOU DECIDE Choose an activity.

1. **Work independently.** Think of another use for an ROV. Draw and label your idea. Share it with the class.

2. **Work in pairs.** Imagine you're an underwater archaeologist. What do you like about the job? What don't you like about it? Discuss your ideas with a partner.

3. **Work in groups.** Make a list of five unusual jobs. Ask students in your class which of the jobs they would like to do. Ask them to explain their answers.

Extending the conversation

Topic	Extending the conversation
I'd like to be an explorer.	And you? What about you? What do you think?
I can speak Spanish.	Can you?
He knows how to dive.	Do you?

1 **Listen.** How do the speakers extend the conversation? Write the phrases you hear. 🎧 022

2 **Read and complete the dialogue.**

Elena: I'd love to work on a cruise ship and travel the world.

_____

Sarah: Not me. The travelling would be fun, but I think it's *really* hard work.

_____

Elena: You're right, it may be hard work. But I like exploring new places.

_____

Sarah: I do, but remember, you have to look after people. It's not a holiday!

Elena: You're right, but I love people, so it's OK. And I speak Spanish, English and Mandarin, so I can talk to people from lots of different places.

_____

Sarah: No, I can only speak English. You know, I think I'll be a travel writer. That way, I can travel without looking after other people!

3 **Work in pairs.** Spin the wheel. Read the sentence aloud, giving correct information about yourself. Then extend the conversation.

> It would be really cool to work in an airport. What do you think?

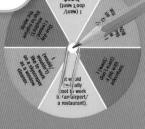

4 **Discuss in pairs.** How does this strategy help you to communicate better? What are some other words or phrases you know that will help you learn more about the person you're talking to?

Go to page 155.

GRAMMAR 🎧 023

Present simple questions and answers: Talking about routines

Does a pastry chef **wear** a uniform?   **Yes**, he **does**. / **No**, he **doesn't**.

Do pastry chefs **work** every day?   **Yes**, they **do**. / **No**, they **don't**.

How do you **create** beautiful desserts?   I **plan** the design. Then I **find** the right ingredients.

Where do pastry chefs **work**?   We **work** in places like bakeries, restaurants, hotels and cruise ships.

1 **Listen.** You will hear questions that begin with each of the words below. Match the answers to each question word. Write the letter. 🎧 024

| _____ do | _____ how | _____ what | _____ when | _____ where | _____ who |

a. design beautiful desserts

b. in a hotel

c. from 4.30 to 11.30 a.m.

d. six days a week

e. in a restaurant

f. a lot of different tools

g. eat a lot of pastries

h. two other pastry chefs

i. from 6.30 to 11.30 p.m.

j. every day

2 **Read.** Then write the questions. Use the words in brackets.

Gabi: Maria, _____ (where/your brother/work)

Maria: He works at the Ithaa Undersea Restaurant in the Maldives.

Gabi: Undersea restaurant! Cool! _____ (what/he/do)

Maria: He's a waiter. It's amazing. He works *in* the ocean.

Gabi: Wow! _____ each day? (how many people/he/wait on)

Maria: Not many – only 14 people can eat there at one time.

Gabi: _____ often? (do/he/come home)

Maria: No, he doesn't. He usually stays in the Maldives for his holiday.

3 **LEARN NEW WORDS Exploration Cruises is looking for new employees.** Listen to their advert. Read the information. Then listen and repeat. 🎧 025 026

Jobs at Exploration Cruises

Do you want to:

- travel the world for free?
- spend time at sea?
- meet people from all over the world?
- have free meals and accommodation?

We're looking for:

- entertainers
- pastry chefs
- nurses
- waiters

To become an **employee:**

- **Apply for** the job you want.
- If we call you, check your **schedule**.
- Choose a time for an **interview** in your city.
- If we call you back, prepare to show your **skills** on the ship.

ISLAND PRINCESS

4 **Listen.** You will hear an interview with the captain of a cruise ship. Write sentences to answer the questions. 🎧 027

1. How many employees work on the ship?

   _____

2. What is the captain's schedule like?

   _____

3. What is one skill the captain has?

   _____

4. Does the captain like his job?

   _____

5. Does the captain work all year round?

   _____

5 **Work in pairs.** Think of two other questions to ask the captain about his routine. Role-play the rest of the interview.

1 BEFORE YOU READ **Think about this unit's topic.** You will read about two people. Predict what you'll learn about them.

2 LEARN NEW WORDS **Find these words in the reading.** Look at each word's ending. Which of the words are professions? How do you know? Then listen and repeat. ∩ 028

| advisor | commute | create | photographer | scientist |

3 WHILE YOU READ **Look for similarities and differences.** ∩ 029

4 AFTER YOU READ **Work in pairs to answer the questions.**

1. What are Jimmy Chin's three jobs?

2. Jimmy enjoys travelling. How do you know this from the text?

3. Do you think a lot of people visit the places that Jimmy photographs? Why or why not?

4. Why does Kevin go to northern Alaska and the Arctic Ocean?

5. Other than being a planetary scientist, what other job does Kevin have?

Adventures
Near and Far

These explorers love working in extreme places.

You're more likely to find photographer Jimmy Chin commuting to Mount Everest than to an office. Not only is he a photographer, he's also a professional climber and skier. He takes photographs and videos in some of the most amazing – but dangerous – places on Earth.

Jimmy has climbed and photographed the world's highest mountains in Nepal, Tibet and Pakistan. And he does all of this while carrying heavy cameras. Why does Jimmy do such difficult work in such extreme places? 'Creating films and photographs in situations that few others could experience is my life's inspiration,' he says.

Jimmy isn't the only explorer working in extreme places. Planetary scientist Kevin Hand drills through the ice in northern Alaska and the Arctic Ocean to study microscopic life in the water underneath it. He hopes that studying microscopic life under ice on Earth will help him to find and study life under the ice on Jupiter's moon, Europa.

Not all of Kevin's work is in cold, faraway places, though. He also works with directors as a science advisor for films, such as *Europa Report*. Kevin has even been in a film! He was a featured scientist in the film *Aliens of the Deep*.

Jimmy and Kevin make it clear that work doesn't have to be boring!

Jimmy Chin in Yosemite National Park, California, USA

5 **Work in pairs.** Compare and contrast Jimmy Chin and Kevin Hand.

6 **Discuss in groups.**

1. Jimmy and Kevin take risks doing their work. Would you want a job where you had to take risks? Do you think it's good or bad to take risks? Why?

2. Do you think it's important to explore outer space? Why or why not?

VIDEO ▶

Jónína and a team member explore Iceland's underwater fissures.

1 BEFORE YOU WATCH **Discuss in pairs.**

1. Look at the photo. What do you think the divers are looking for? List three ideas.

2. Imagine you're diving in this fissure. Describe what you see.

2 **Work in pairs.** You're going to watch *Searching for Life in Iceland's Fissures*. In this video, you'll see scientists enter the water of an underground fissure in Iceland. Predict a problem they might have.

3 WHILE YOU WATCH **Check your prediction from Activity 2.** Watch scene 2.1.

4 AFTER YOU WATCH **Work in pairs.** Answer the questions below.

1. How did Jónína feel the first time she dived in a fissure? Why?

2. What were Jónína and her team the first to do?

3. Why is it risky to dive in the fissure?

4. Why does it seem that there isn't much living in the waters?

5. How do scientists get the material off the walls of the fissures?

6. What do the scientists do with the samples they collect underwater?

7. What are Jónína's two passions?

5 **Work in pairs.** Both Jónína and Guillermo de Anda are underwater explorers. How are their jobs similar? How are they different? Write your ideas in a Venn diagram.

6 **Work in pairs.** In the video, Jónína says, 'So far, we made some exciting discoveries of species that no one knew existed in Iceland.' Why is it important to discover new information about an animal species? Give an example of what can be learnt from new discoveries.

7 **YOU DECIDE** **Choose an activity.**

1. **Work independently.** What things other than animals can we study underwater? List three things and give an example of what we could learn from each one.

2. **Work in pairs.** Research another job that combines diving and science. Imagine you have that job. Explain your job to the class.

3. **Work in groups.** Find out about a person from your country who recently discovered something unusual. Prepare a profile of this person. Present it to the class.

Possessives: Showing ownership

This **dentist's** job isn't done in an office.

Dr Perkins's job is to get the equipment on the plane.

Pilots' days are very long.

My job is helping ill people. What's **your** job?

The flying dentist thinks **her** job is great. The pilot likes **his** job, too. The job also has **its** advantages.

In **our** job, we help everyone, no matter what **their** problem is.

1 **Read.** Circle the possessives.

My name is Dr Smith, and I'm a flight dentist with the Royal Flying Doctor Service of Australia (RFDS). Its 63 planes fly every day of the year. Our goal is to deliver health services to people in rural areas.

I work with a great team. Our days are very long, but no two days are ever the same. One doctor on the team says that he loves his job because it's never boring! I don't have an office so I check patients' teeth in their homes. This morning I checked Ms Lee's teeth in her living room and the Watson family's teeth on their porch!

2 **Work independently.** Interview classmates to learn about jobs that their family and friends have. Put an X over the job when you find a classmate who knows someone with that job. Play until you cross out five jobs. Then report to the class using possessives.

Is someone in your family an engineer?

Yes, my uncle is an engineer! He loves his job.

restaurant employee	writer	programmer	teacher
office worker	engineer	construction worker	doctor or nurse

WRITING

A descriptive paragraph should include the following:

Title: Gives an idea of what the paragraph is about
Topic sentence: Is usually the first sentence; says what the paragraph is about
Details: Give more information about the topic sentence
Concluding sentence: Ends the paragraph

1 **Read the model.** Work in pairs to identify the title, topic sentence, details and concluding sentence. Underline each part.

A Typical Work Day

My aunt has a great job at an orangutan sanctuary. She's the daytime babysitter for a five-month-old orangutan called Coco. Coco's mother died, so they need to take care of her 24 hours a day. When my aunt arrives in the morning, she gives Coco milk in her bottle and changes her nappy. She does this several times a day. Then she works as Coco's teacher, teaching her the skills she needs for living in the forest, such as climbing. Coco likes climbing up, but not down! She screams for my aunt's help sometimes. My aunt hugs her when she gets scared. In the early evening, it's Coco's bedtime, and their time together that day is over. My aunt puts Coco to bed and goes home. My aunt says, 'I love Coco, and I love my job!'

2 **Work in pairs.** What is unusual about the orangutan babysitter's job? Would you like to have this job? Why or why not?

3 **Write.** Describe the daily routine of someone you know who has an unusual job. Include a title, a topic sentence, details and a concluding sentence.

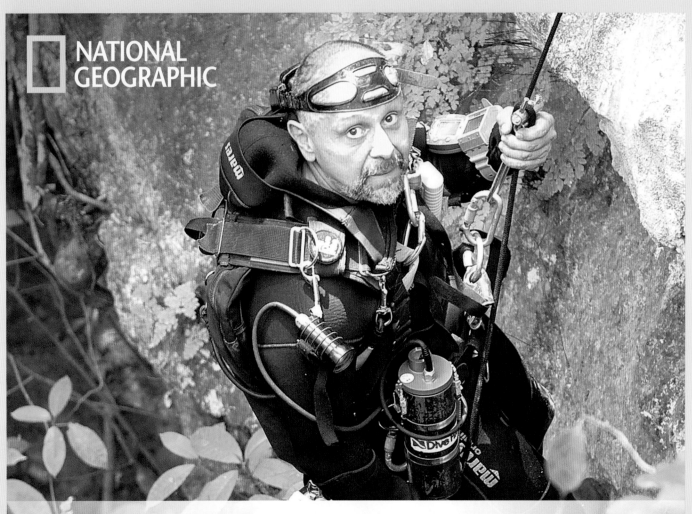

Do What You Love

'I have the coolest job in the world because I love what I do!'

Guillermo de Anda
National Geographic Explorer, Underwater Archaeologist

1. **Watch scene 2.2.**

2. Guillermo loved diving from a very young age. How do you think this helped him to choose a career? How does he combine his love of diving with his love of science?

3. What career do you want to have? What will you need to do to prepare for this career? If you choose this career, will you be doing what you love? Explain.

Make an Impact

1 Write a job advert.

- Imagine you own a company and you need someone for an unusual job.
- Create a job advert. Write a description of the job. Include information about your company.
- Share your job advert with the class. Is anyone interested in your unusual job? Interview them for the job!

2 Create a comic strip.

- Interview a person who has a typical job. Ask this person to mention three or four unusual or unexpected parts of the job.
- Design a comic strip to illustrate the unusual aspects of this person's job.
- Share your comic strip with the class.

3 Plan a job fair for unusual jobs.

- Find information about five interesting and unusual careers.
- Make posters showing a typical day for these workers.
- Display the posters in your classroom. Talk to your classmates about what each job involves.

Express Yourself

1 Read and listen to the online travel review. 🎧 031

GoTravel REVIEWS

GONDOLA TOURS OF VENICE

🧳🧳🧳🧳🗎 **210 reviews**

🧳🧳🧳🧳🧳 JGirl, Seoul

'Our gondolier saved my holiday!'

Well, I'm in Venice, Italy, with my family! Venice is incredible! The city is hundreds of years old, and it's built on WATER. People get around on special boats called *gondolas*, and today I had my first gondola ride!

A gondolier controls the gondola using an oar and his own strength. (These gondoliers are REALLY strong.) The gondolier's job is to describe Venice's culture and history as he takes you through the city's canals. Our gondolier was so good at telling stories I almost forgot I was sharing the ride with my parents.

That might sound exciting, and it was, but of course I was with ... my dad. And Dad thought it would be funny to wear a striped shirt to match the gondolier's shirt. How *embarrassing*!

My parents loved looking at the beautiful bridges, churches and palaces along the route. I really enjoyed listening to our gondolier talk about his work. He told us that it takes years of study and practice to get the job. Who knew? He also told us that of all the gondoliers in Venice, only one is a woman! I think I need to change that! It's time to start training for my dream job! Maybe my dad will let me borrow his shirt. ;)

Gondola Tours of Venice gave me a great tour of a beautiful city – and an interesting idea for my future career! I recommend the gondola tour to anyone who's interested in learning about unusual places and unusual jobs ... especially if they're stuck on a boat with their parents!

2 Work in groups. Discuss the review.

1. Does JGirl's review make you want to visit Venice and go on a gondola ride? Why or why not?

2. Do you think the review gives enough information? Is it funny and interesting? What else would you like to know about Venice or about Gondola Tours of Venice?

3 Connect ideas. In Unit 1, you learnt about exploring and unusual places. In Unit 2, you learnt about unusual jobs. What connection can you see between the two units?

Gondolas in Venice, Italy

4 YOU DECIDE Choose an activity.

1. Choose a topic:
   - an unusual place
   - an unusual job

2. Choose a way to express yourself:
   - a review
   - an advertisement
   - an interview

3. Present your work.

Secrets of the Dark

'To me, science is fiction because sometimes it just seems unreal. Looking at bioluminescence, it's just beautiful. It's artwork.'

David Gruber

Blue ghost fireflies

TO START

1. In the photo, fireflies create a beautiful light. What other things in nature produce light?

2. Bioluminescent animals use lights to communicate with one another. How do humans use lights to communicate?

3. Where do you feel comfortable in the dark? Why?

1 **What would be difficult about living without sunlight for two months every year?** Discuss. Then listen and read. 🎧 **032**

For most of us, the days are divided into day and night. But for two months each winter in northern Norway, it's **dark** for 20 hours a day. There is no **sunrise** or **sunset** because the sun never gets above the **horizon**.

Would you like to live in **darkness** for this long? It may seem difficult, but many Norwegians love the beautiful colours of these months. To the **south** are the red and gold colours of the horizon. To the **north**, the sky is a magnificent blue. Even the moon and stars look blue. In the towns, streetlights shine like little yellow diamonds.

People do need light to be healthy and happy. Since they don't have much daylight during this time of the year, Norwegians

In the town of Longyearbyen, in northern Norway, there's no sunlight from November to January. However, the sun doesn't set from the end of April to the end of August.

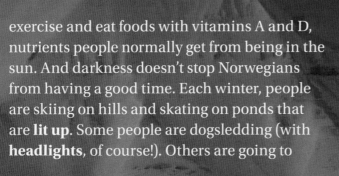

exercise and eat foods with vitamins A and D, nutrients people normally get from being in the sun. And darkness doesn't stop Norwegians from having a good time. Each winter, people are skiing on hills and skating on ponds that are **lit up**. Some people are dogsledding (with **headlights**, of course!). Others are going to film and music **festivals**. And other people are spending time with friends in cafés and restaurants. Of course, not everyone is so **active** in the dark months. Many people are just **going to sleep** a little earlier until the sun returns in the spring.

2 LEARN NEW WORDS **Listen and repeat.** ⌒**033**

3 **Work in pairs.** What would you like about living in the dark for two months? What wouldn't you like? Write three things for each. Compare your list with your partner's.

4 Read and write the words from the list. Make any necessary changes.

active	dark	darkness	festival	go to sleep
headlight	light up	south	sunrise	sunset

Light and _____ are two things we don't often think about. This is because we can have light any time at night. Thanks to electric lights, we're able to do what we need to at night. We _____ because we're tired, not just because it's _____ . 'Having all this energy to be able to have light at night is a really new thing for humans,' says scientist David Gruber. Until the 19th century, people didn't have lights like we do today. The light of day came from the sun, as it does now. But at night, only the light of the moon and the stars _____ the sky. People got up at _____ and were _____ all day. Then, after _____ , they went to bed.

5 LEARN NEW WORDS Listen to these words. Match each word to its definition. Then listen and repeat. 🎧 034 035

daylight	healthy	streetlight

_____ 1. a light near a road

_____ 2. not ill

_____ 3. light from the sun

A kinkajou

6 YOU DECIDE Choose an activity.

1. **Work independently.** Observe an animal at night. What do you notice? What is surprising? Write your findings. Share them with the class.

2. **Work in pairs.** Imagine you lived hundreds of years ago. How was your life at night different from your life at night now? List at least five examples.

3. **Work in groups.** When you haven't got electric light, what can you use to help you see in the dark? List three things. Choose one thing from your list and make an advertisement for it. Present your advert to the class.

Asking for help with schoolwork	Helping with schoolwork
What does *nocturnal* mean?	It means *active at night*.
How do you pronounce it?	I'm not sure. I think you say *nock-tur-null*.
How do you spell it?	It's spelt *n-o-c-t-u-r-n-a-l*.

1. **Listen.** How do the speakers ask for help and respond? Write the phrases you hear. 🎧 037

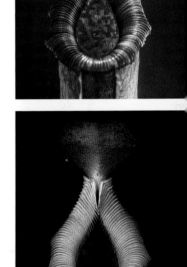

2. **Read and complete the dialogue.**

Mae: This video about carnivorous plants is really cool.

Hwan: _____

Mae: _____ *things that eat meat.* This one is called a *Nepenthes*.

Hwan: What? _____

Mae: _____ Let's look it up. *N-e-p-e-n-t-h-e-s.* Another name is *pitcher plant*. It eats arthropods.

Hwan: Arthro ... what? _____

Mae: _____ *ar-throw-pod.* You know, insects, spiders and things like that. Insects see the plant's light and go to it. Then they fall inside and die! That's how the plant eats them.

Hwan: Amazing!

A glowing pitcher plant

3. **Work in pairs.** Talk about the animals on the cards. Help your partner to spell, pronounce and learn more about each animal.

It's a Gila monster.

A *what*? How do you pronounce that?

Go to page 157.

4. **Work in groups.** Think of a situation where you wanted to ask for help with schoolwork but didn't. Why didn't you ask? How can knowing these phrases help you in the future?

GRAMMAR ⌂ 038

Present continuous: Saying what is happening now

Non-action verbs	Action verbs
I **like** stories about unusual animals.	While I**'m reading** in bed at night in Mexico, my friend Akiko **is reading** at school in Japan!
Many animals **see** well enough to hunt in the dark.	While some animals **are hunting** in the dark, others **are hiding** or **sleeping**.
It **is** 2.00 a.m. in the jungle, but that doesn't **mean** all the animals **are** asleep.	The monkeys **are sleeping** in trees, but the kinkajous **are looking** for food.

1 **Listen.** Circle the non-action verbs you hear. Underline the action verbs you hear. ⌂ 039

bake	be	drive	enjoy	fly	help
know	like	need	open	search	sleep

2 **Read and complete the sentences.** Use the *–ing* ending for action verbs.

1. People _____ (agree) that it's good to spend time with family.

2. This is difficult for family members who _____ (live) in different countries.

3. It's difficult because of different time zones. This _____ (mean) that it might be morning in one place and afternoon in another.

4. For example, Omar in Santiago _____ (eat) breakfast while his cousin Ali in Dubai _____ (come) home from school.

5. So when Ali _____ (think) about calling Omar, he _____ (have) to consider the time in Santiago first.

3 **Work in pairs.** Write what you do at these times. Compare your answers with a partner.

> If it's Monday night, I'm studying, but Julia is making dinner.

	Me	_____
Monday night		
Wednesday during school		
Friday evening		
Saturday afternoon		
Sunday morning		

4 **LEARN NEW WORDS** **Listen to learn about time zones.** Then listen and repeat. 🎧 **040 041**

World **Time Zones**

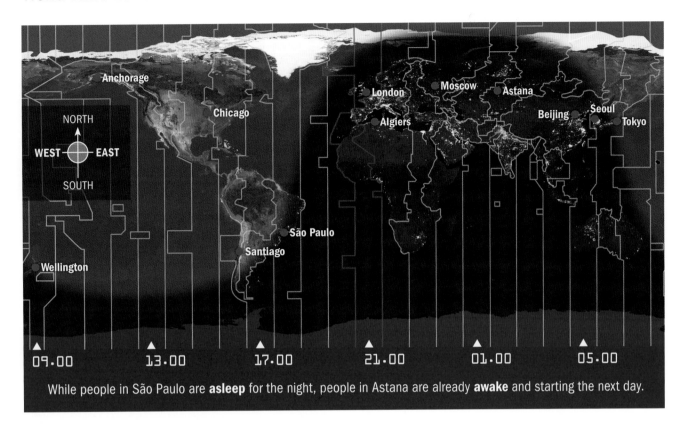

09.00   13.00   17.00   21.00   01.00   05.00

While people in São Paulo are **asleep** for the night, people in Astana are already **awake** and starting the next day.

5 **Work in pairs.** Find these cities and their time zones on the map. How many time zones separate them? Write a sentence about what people might be doing in each city.

1. Seoul / Santiago *There are 13 time zones between Seoul and Santiago. While people in Santiago are coming home from school and work, people in Seoul are asleep.*

2. Anchorage / London _____

3. São Paulo / Tokyo _____

4. Chicago / London _____

6 **Work in groups.** Find the place where you live on the map. Note the time now. Choose three other cities. Say if they are to your east or west and what time it is there. Take turns comparing what you're doing with what people in those cities are probably doing.

1 **BEFORE YOU READ Discuss in pairs.** What do you know about the ocean and life in the ocean? What do you want to learn?

2 **Look at the text and photos quickly.** Then answer the questions.

1. Who is this reading about?
2. What sea animal has got really big eyes?

3 **LEARN NEW WORDS Find the words in the text.** Guess their meaning. Then look at the first meaning given for each word in the dictionary. Compare those meanings with your guesses. Then listen and repeat. 🎧 **042**

| dawn | fascinate | glow | observe | pattern |

4 **WHILE YOU READ Think about what makes animals in the deep ocean different.** 🎧 **043**

5 **AFTER YOU READ Work in pairs.** Tick T for *true* or F for *false*.

1. David observes life in the ocean when it's dark. **(T✓)** **(F)**

2. We know a lot about everything that lives in the ocean. **(T)** **(F✓)**

3. We can see all the glowing colours in the ocean with our eyes. **(T)** **(F✓)**

4. Only one type of animal glows in the dark through the lens of David's camera. **(T)** **(F✓)**

5. A lot of animals at the bottom of the ocean make their own light. **(T✓)** **(F)**

6. The vampire squid has very large eyes to help it see in the dark. **(T✓)** **(F)**

6 **Review.** Look at your answers from Activity 2. Were they correct? What else did you learn about the person and the sea animal?

A shark glows bright green through the filters of David's camera.

There are incredible creatures living in the darkness.

In the darkness before dawn, marine biologist David Gruber dives into the ocean to observe the amazing creatures that live there. 'Seventy-one per cent of Earth is ocean, and much of it is dark, with tonnes of life down there that we don't know about,' he says.

David discovered that many sea animals can see colours in the water that we cannot. So he designed a camera that allows him to see the colours just as a fish does. His camera shows a secret world of neon green, red and orange colours on ocean life that glows in the dark.

In this fascinating world, David discovered a special kind of shark that glows bright with green spots. 'When you see all these little bright spots and patterns, it's like flowers and butterflies. Why do they make patterns? It's to attract each other. It's to recognise each other,' he says.

At the bottom of the ocean where there is no light at all, many animals produce their own light. The unusual vampire squid is an example. It can turn itself on or off, just like a lamp. It also has very big eyes to help it see in the dark. In fact, compared to its body size, the vampire squid has the largest eyes of any animal in the world. And this is just one animal: ninety per cent of the animals that live at the bottom of the ocean produce their own light.

It's easy to see why the darkness of the sea fascinates David. 'Marine animals in the dark ocean produce lights to communicate with each other,' says David. 'It's an underwater disco party. We human beings are the last ones to join in!'

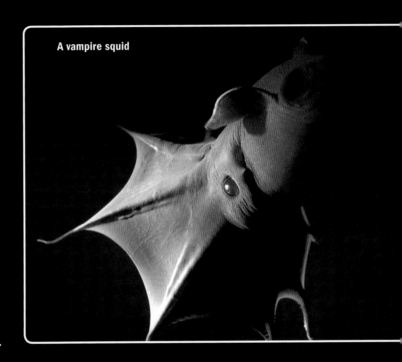

A vampire squid

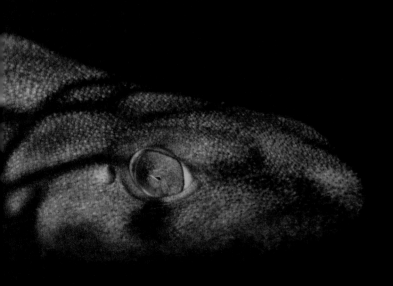

7 **Discuss in groups.**

1. What things about the ocean fascinate you? Why do they fascinate you?

2. It's difficult to study the ocean at night because of the darkness. What are some other difficulties David might have when studying the ocean at night?

3. Do you think it's important to learn about what lives in the ocean? Why or why not?

VIDEO ▷

1 **BEFORE YOU WATCH Discuss in pairs.**

1. What did you love doing as a small child? Do you still love it? What else do you love doing now?

2. Are you interested in learning about what's in the ocean? Why or why not?

2 **Work in pairs.** The title of the video you're going to watch is *What Glows Beneath*. Think of what you have learnt about David Gruber and his work. Then make two lists: *What I have learnt about David* and *What I want to learn about David.*

3 **WHILE YOU WATCH Circle the correct answers.** Watch scene 3.1.

> 1. David first became fascinated by the ocean by *surfing / scuba diving.*
>
> 2. David wondered *if it would be hard to study biology / what was beneath him in the water.*
>
> 3. David wanted to photograph the ocean so that he can *sell his photos to magazines / understand how fish see it.*
>
> 4. David says that *there's still a lot to learn about / scientists have discovered all of the species of* the ocean.
>
> 5. According to David, the future of exploration is finding out *why humans don't glow / how humans fit in among nature.*

AFTER YOU WATCH Work in pairs to answer the questions.

1. What was David's hobby when he was a teenager?
2. How does this hobby connect to his job?
3. What is special about how David studies the ocean?
4. What do the filters in David's camera allow him to do?

⑤ **Work in pairs.** List three of the sea animals you saw in the video. Describe what they look like. Now think of three sea animals you know about or have seen photos of. How are they different from the animals in the video?

David uses a camera with special filters to explore the dark ocean.

⑥ **YOU DECIDE Choose an activity.**

1. **Work independently.** Imagine that you went scuba diving and saw some of the animals in the video. Write a postcard to a friend or family member, describing what you saw. In your postcard, explain how you were able to see the animals glow.

2. **Work in pairs.** Role-play a conversation between David and a reporter who's asking him about his work. Share your dialogue with the class.

3. **Work in groups.** Prepare a glow-in-the-dark presentation. Each person finds out about a different sea animal that glows in the dark. Draw it or find a photo of it. Write three pieces of information about it. Present your group of animals to the class.

At, on and in: Saying when things happen

at eight o'clock / **at** night / **at** the weekend
on Monday(s) / **on** 1st June / **on** my birthday
in the winter / **in** the morning / **in** 2017 / **in** May

1 **Read.** Complete the paragraph with *at, on* or *in.*

My family and I visited Marrakesh, Morocco, _____ 2015. We went _____ December. The weather is warm there _____ the winter. _____ Monday, our first day, we spent a lot of time in the Jemaa el Fna, the old city square. _____ lunchtime, we ate at a rooftop café, and _____ the afternoon, we watched some dancers. _____ five o'clock _____ the evening, we watched the day market stalls leave and the night market stalls arrive. _____ night we enjoyed the storytellers, magicians, musicians and acrobats, as well as the food from the many food stalls. The Jemaa el Fna is incredible both day and night!

The Jemaa el Fna market

2 **Work in pairs.** Talk about places you go to regularly. Use *at, on* and *in.*

1. Tuesdays _____ *On Tuesdays, I go to the park after school.* _____

2. night _____

3. afternoon _____

4. March _____

5. weekend _____

6. 8.00 a.m. _____

3 **Work in pairs.** Take turns throwing the cube. Talk about things that happen at different times.

> In the summer, we often go to the beach.

Go to page 159.

WRITING

In sensory writing, we choose a topic such as an event or a place. We use adjectives, or describing words, to explain what we see, hear, taste, smell and feel. Describing something using senses helps our reader imagine that he or she is at that event or place.

1 Read the model. Work in pairs to identify and underline the words that describe what people see, hear, taste, smell and feel.

When thousands of glowing lanterns light up the city at night on the 15th day of the Chinese New Year, I know the Chinese Lantern Festival has arrived. All kinds of lanterns shine brightly against the dark night sky. Some of the lanterns are small, and others are really big. Some look like beautiful flowers and dragons. The silk lanterns feel soft. The plastic lanterns feel smooth and warm. Families walk happily in the crowded streets, looking at the many kinds of amazing lanterns. While some people are enjoying the colourful lanterns, others are watching exciting parades and traditional Chinese lion dance performances. The loud, popping sounds of firecrackers fill the air. People prepare tasty rice dumplings in the morning for their families and friends to enjoy in the evening. The sweet smell makes me hungry for my favourite food. I love everything about this night-time festival.

A Lantern Festival celebration
in Shanghai, China

2 Work in pairs. Can you imagine how it feels to be at the Chinese Lantern Festival? Why or why not?

3 Write. Describe a fun night-time event. Use sensory words to say what you see, hear, taste, smell and feel at this event.

Understand and Protect

'People want to protect things they love and understand. The more I can share about the amazing animals I get to explore, the more people may want to help protect them.'

David Gruber
National Geographic Explorer, Marine Biologist

1. **Watch scene 3.2.**

2. David cares deeply about the ocean and ocean life. Why is it important to protect animals in the ocean? How does David's work help protect them?

3. What do you want to protect? Why? How can you get others to care about this?

Make an Impact

YOU DECIDE Choose a project.

1 **Design a poster.**

· Research animals or plants that glow in the dark. Find out how and why they glow.

· Make a poster to describe three of the glow-in-the-dark organisms you researched. Include photos.

· Present your poster to the class.

2 **Write a blog entry.**

· Research a place that is light for more than two months a year.

· Pretend that you visit during the light season. Write a blog about your visit. Include photos.

· Publish your blog. Answer questions and respond to your classmates' comments.

3 **Make a 'day-and-night' video.**

· Choose an interesting place in your region.

· Make a video of that place during the day and during the night. Mention what is the same and what is different.

· Share your video with the class.

Bioluminescent fungi glowing
on a tree trunk

Living Together

'Let's think about what we can do today to make sure our grandchildren have the option of seeing wildlife in the future.'
Amy Dickman

A rhinoceros and its caretaker
at a conservancy in Kenya

TO START

1. What's happening in the photo? How do you think the man feels? The animal?

2. What are situations where people and animals live together peacefully? What are situations where they don't get along?

3. Do you think that seeing wild animals where they live is a good idea? Why or why not?

1 **Why might baboons and humans come into contact with each other?** Discuss. Then listen and read. 🎧 045

Human-**wildlife conflict** is a big problem all over the world today, and it's getting bigger. Imagine finding a baboon or two eating breakfast at your table! That would definitely be a conflict between a human, you, and wildlife, the baboons! Because baboons are **wild**, this type of conflict could be dangerous.

In Cape Town, South Africa, humans are **interacting** with baboons more than ever, right in their own neighbourhoods. Because about half of the natural baboon **habitat** and food in this region **disappeared**, baboons needed to find new ways to get food. So they started going into urban areas and stealing the food they need for survival.

A family of baboons at the breakfast table

Baboons are very **clever** animals. Once they **learn** that they can easily get food from humans, they won't try as hard to hunt for their own food. People who live near baboon habitats have to control this **behaviour** by limiting the baboons' **access** to human food and rubbish.

Both humans and wildlife **need** protection from each other. Luckily, in some places in South Africa, there are people who work as baboon monitors. Their job is to keep baboons away from homes. Because baboons are **afraid of** loud noises, monitors use noise-making devices to **frighten** them away. They might also use paintballs to frighten the baboons.

The monitors don't form relationships with the baboons, but they don't mistreat them either. They simply work to limit conflicts between humans and wildlife.

2 **LEARN NEW WORDS Listen and repeat.** 🎧 046

3 **Work in pairs.** Think about a time when an unwanted animal came into your house. How did you feel? What did you do?

4 Read and circle the correct word.

Amy Dickman is trying to solve *wildlife / conflicts* between humans and the *wild / interacting* big cats in villages around Ruaha National Park in Tanzania. The big cat *habitat / behaviour* in the park is disappearing. As a result, these big cats *frighten / need* to find new ways to get food. So they go onto farms and kill farm animals for food. Because the farmers are *clever / afraid of* losing their animals, they kill the big cats.

Amy is trying to change the *wildlife / behaviour* of villagers toward the big cats. She's also helping villagers find better ways to protect their animals. Amy believes that people should *interact / disappear* with wildlife in ways that give both groups *habitat / access* to the resources they need.

5 LEARN NEW WORDS Listen to these words and complete the sentences. Then listen and repeat. 🎧 047 048

hunt	mistreat	relationship	survival

1. Wild animals _____ for their food.
2. Dogs and their owners have a special _____ .
3. All living things need food and water for their _____ .
4. People who hit animals _____ them.

6 YOU DECIDE Choose an activity. Work in pairs.

1. Discuss. What animals in your country are losing their habitat? What problems do they have? What are people doing about it?

2. Make a list of three reasons why people hunt wild animals. Do you think humans should change their behaviour so that they don't need to hunt?

3. Find a group where you live that works with wild animals. Learn about what they do and why they do it.

A snow leopard

Asking for reasons	Giving reasons
Why <u>are villagers afraid of wild animals</u>?	Because <u>they're dangerous</u>.
<u>Farmers need to protect their animals from wild animals</u>. Do you know why?	It's because <u>wild animals hunt farm animals for food</u>.
<u>Wild animals are interacting with people more often</u>. Why is that?	Since <u>their habitats are disappearing, they're going where humans live</u>.

1 **Listen.** How do the speakers ask for and give reasons? Write the words and phrases you hear. ∩050

2 **Read and complete the dialogue.**

Abdul: Look at this picture of people on an Indian tiger reserve.

Anna: The people are wearing masks. _____

Abdul: _____ they're trying to trick the tigers.

Anna: They're wearing the masks on the *backs* of their heads!
   _____

Abdul: _____ tigers attack people from behind, they see the mask and think the person is looking at them. That scares them.

Anna: Incredible! But _____ do people go onto the tiger reserve?

Abdul: _____ they fish there. They also collect honey and wood in the reserves.

Anna: So the people wear masks _____ they believe the masks will protect them from tigers?

Abdul: That's right. In three years, tigers only attacked people who weren't wearing masks!

Anna: Wow! Tigers are clever, though. They might soon learn that people are tricking them.

Why are there baboon monitors in Cape Town?

Baboons go into urban areas. Monitors help to keep them away from humans.

3 **Work in pairs.** Take a card and read the sentence. Ask your partner for the reason. Your partner will answer the question. Then swap roles.

4 **Work in pairs.** Talk about animals. Talk about three problems, interesting facts or interactions. Your partner will ask for reasons. Respond and then swap roles.

There are baboon monitors in Cape Town.

Go to page 161.

Modals: Describing obligation and advice

Necessary	We **must** learn more about the fight to save rhinos.
	We **have to** protect rhinos.
Not necessary	We **don't have to** use products made from rhinoceros horn.
Recommended	We **shouldn't** ignore the rhino problem.
	Everyone **should** do something, even if it's a small action.

RHINOCEROS POPULATIONS WORLDWIDE

20,405 WHITE RHINO

5,055 BLACK RHINO

3,333 GREATER ONE-HORNED RHINO

<100

58–60 SUMATRAN RHINO

① **Listen.** How can we save rhinos? Complete the sentences. Then tick the correct box. 🎧 052

	necessary	not necessary	recommended
1. Rangers _____ go into the rhino areas and catch the hunters.	☐	☐	☐
2. Rhino monitors _____ know when rhino babies are born.	☐	☐	☐
3. We _____ use rhino horn in medicine.	☐	☐	☐
4. We _____ keep some rhinos in protected places to have babies safely.	☐	☐	☐
5. We _____ save rhinos ourselves.	☐	☐	☐

② **Work in pairs.** Listen again to the passage. Write two additional ways to save rhinos. Say if they are *necessary*, *not necessary* or *recommended*. 🎧 053

1. _____

2. _____

3 **Work in pairs.** Give advice on how people can protect wildlife. Use *must, (don't) have to, should* and *shouldn't.*

> We shouldn't hunt wild animals just for fun.

> You're right. And we must stop hunters that hunt for fur.

4 **LEARN NEW WORDS Listen to learn about saving sea turtles.** Then listen and repeat. 🎧 054 055

Saving Sea Turtles

Humans are sea turtles' biggest **predator**.

Sea turtle eggs are **prey** for seagulls as well as humans.

Sea turtles cannot **defend** themselves against humans.

The Turtle Hospital in Florida, USA, **rescues injured** sea turtles.

Sea turtles have to survive. We must all do something to help them.

5 **Work independently.** Think of another wild animal that is endangered. Write about why it's endangered. Give advice on how to protect it. Remember to use *must, (don't) have to, should* and *shouldn't.*

_____

_____

_____

_____

6 **Work in groups.** Imagine you work for a group that helps protect sea turtles. What five pieces of advice would you give people on what to do?

> We must help people who sell eggs find other ways to make money.

1 **BEFORE YOU READ** **Discuss in pairs.** What does it mean to be an animal hero? What do you want to learn about the animal heroes?

2 **LEARN NEW WORDS** **Find these words in the text.** Look for words that appear together, such as *domestic animals*. Then listen and repeat. ∩ 056

| avoid | chemical | domestic | feeling | sniff |

3 **WHILE YOU READ** **Look for problems and solutions.** ∩ 057

4 **AFTER YOU READ** **Work in pairs to answer the questions.**

1. What is Bart Weetjen's organisation? What does it do?
2. Why does Bart think that rats are heroes?
3. How do landmines make life hard for farmers and villagers?
4. What lifesaving skill do dogs have?
5. What is one thing that both rats and dogs can do?

H FOUR-LEGGED
Heroes

Animals with Amazing Abilities

Most people have mixed feelings about rats and avoid them if they can. Bart Weetjens thinks that we must treat rats as heroes.

Bart started an organisation called APOPO in Tanzania. Bart's organisation trains African giant pouched rats to sniff the ground in order to find underground landmines left in the area during past wars. Many of these landmines are still active. They often explode, killing and injuring thousands of people each year. Villagers avoid places where the dangerous landmines are. But much of this land could be used as valuable farmland if the mines weren't there. These rats are helping villagers get their land back.

The giant rats are never mistreated. None of them die doing their work. They even have sunblock put on their ears and tails while they work. And when they find a landmine, they get a treat!

While rats aren't usually seen as heroes, some domestic animals, like dogs, often are. There are many stories about dogs that save lives, but dogs have another lifesaving skill that we're still learning about. Just like landmine-sniffing rats, dogs have an amazing sense of smell. They're now being trained to sniff out chemicals from the body that are connected to certain diseases, sometimes even before doctors or laboratory tests can find them!

So, the next time you see a rat or dog, don't be afraid. Remember, these animal heroes can save lives.

A medical dog sniffing for diseases

A giant pouched rat sniffing a landmine

5 **Complete the table.** Write two problems and two solutions.

Problem	Solution

6 **Discuss in groups.**

1. Did the reading change your feelings about rats? Dogs? Explain.

2. What other animals do you know about that have helped people or saved lives? How did they help?

3. Imagine you train animals to help people or save lives. What kind of animal would you train? Why? How would it help?

VIDE⯈

1 BEFORE YOU WATCH Discuss in pairs.

1. An orphan elephant is a young elephant without a mother. What do you think happened to the orphans' mothers? Give one or two ideas.

2. Why do you think people have to take care of the young orphan elephants?

2 Read and circle. You're going to watch *The Elephant Whisperers*. Use the title to predict what the video is about. Circle the number.

1. Baby elephants in a zoo

2. Elephant and human conflicts

3. People who take care of baby elephants

3 WHILE YOU WATCH Write two words that describe the elephants and two words that describe the humans. Watch scene 4.1.

Elephants:

_____

_____

Humans:

_____

_____

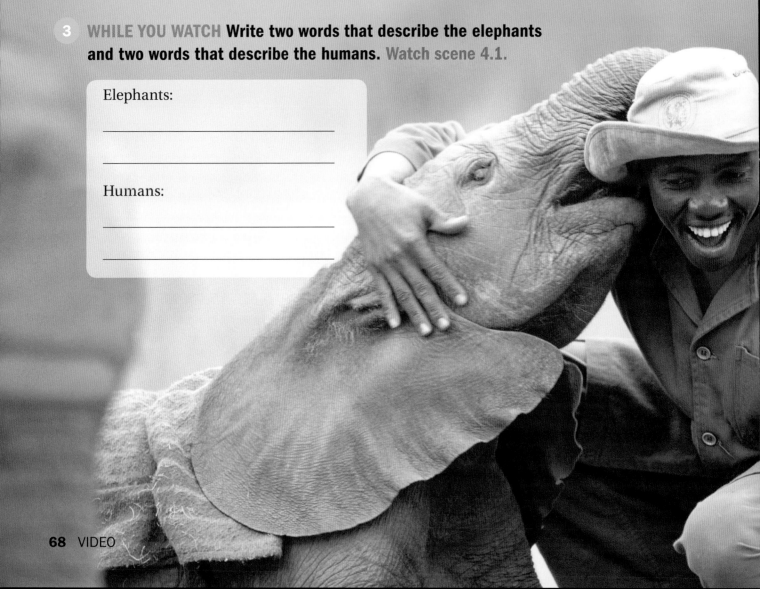

4 **Work in pairs.** Put the daily events in order, according to the video.

_____ The keepers feed and play with the elephants.

_____ The keepers and elephants go back to the camp.

_____ The keepers and elephants go to the bush.

___1___ The elephant keepers get up at 5.30 a.m.

_____ The elephants and their keepers go to bed.

5 **AFTER YOU WATCH** **Read the sentences.** Tick T for *true* or F for *false*.

1. The elephants are not very friendly.   **T**   **F**

2. The elephants are from different places in Kenya.   **T**   **F**

3. The elephants want to be alone.   **T**   **F**

4. The elephants only like to be with their keepers.   **T**   **F**

5. The keepers stay with the elephants at night so that they don't cry.   **T**   **F**

6 **Discuss in pairs.**

1. How are elephants and humans alike? Name three similarities.

2. What do you think is fun about being an elephant keeper? What do you think is hard?

7 **YOU DECIDE** **Choose an activity.**

1. **Work independently.** Imagine you're an elephant keeper. Write a letter to your family explaining a day in your life.

2. **Work in pairs.** Write a job advertisement for an elephant keeper. Describe the job and the type of person needed to do it.

3. **Work in groups.** In the video, you saw workers playing ball with the elephants. Think of at least three other fun ways that humans can interact with elephants. Present your ideas to the class.

Modals: Describing ability in present and past

Many types of wildlife today **can't** cross roads safely.

What **can** we do about it?

We **can** help them by building animal crossings.

In 1987, salamanders **couldn't** safely cross a street in Amherst, Massachusetts, USA.

How **could** they avoid cars?

People built tunnels under the street. This way, the salamanders **could** cross safely.

1 **Read.** Complete the paragraph with *can, can't, could* or *couldn't.*

Roads _____ be dangerous for both humans and wildlife. Roads go though wildlife habitat, so animals _____ cross safely. When cars hit animals, people _____ get hurt, too.

This is changing now in many countries. Before 2011, elephants _____ safely cross a road in Kenya. But now they _____ because the government built a tunnel under the road.

On Christmas Island in Australia, cars killed around 500,000 red crabs every year. People thought of ways they _____ help the crabs. They built special bridges over the road. Now the crabs _____ be harmed because they _____ climb over the bridges to safety.

In Holland, people knew they _____ help their wildlife stay alive. So they worked to create over 600 animal crossings. Now wildlife and people _____ travel where they need to go safely.

2 **Work in pairs.** Play Noughts and Crosses. Describe your own abilities now and in the past. Mark X or O. Try to get three in a row.

> When I was six, I couldn't teach my dog to do tricks.

can	coⓍln't	could
could	**wild**	can't
couldn't	can	can't

Go to page 159.

WRITING

After you write, re-read your paragraph. Make sure it's organised and clear. When you have a good draft, proofread your paragraph. Make a note of spelling, grammar and punctuation mistakes. Then rewrite the paragraph, correcting the mistakes.

1 **Read the model.** Underline the spelling mistakes in the paragraph. Circle the grammar mistakes.

Wong Siew Te at the Bornean Sun Bear Conservation Centre in Malaysia felt both sad and happy the day he take Natalie, a sun bear, back to her natural home in the forrest. Hunters killed Natalie's mother when she was a baby, so she couldn't do everything bears need for servivel in a forest. Te took care of her for almost five years. He cared for her like a duaghter. He teached Natalie how to live like a wild bear. For example, he teached her how to find food and build nests. Te knew he can't keep Natalie at the reserve forever because sun bears belong in the forest. When she was. ready, he set her free in the forest. Today he could uses his computer to check on Natalie in her new home. He can do this because she has a specal collar that lets him know where she is. Te and his team is proud they could help Natalie survive in her habitat.

2 **Discuss in pairs.** Do you always read your paragraphs after writing them? What mistakes do you most often make in your writing? How can proofreading help you to become a better writer?

3 **Write.** Write about a special relationship between an animal and a human. Then proofread your paragraph and correct the mistakes.

NATIONAL GEOGRAPHIC

Start Small

'If everyone did something small, it would be huge.'

Amy Dickman
National Geographic Explorer, Animal Conservationist

1. **Watch scene 4.2.**

2. What do you think is the most important thing Amy is doing to help big cats? How does Amy's work help both humans and wildlife?

3. What are some simple things you could do to help protect wildlife? How could it help both humans and animals?

Make an Impact

YOU DECIDE Choose a project.

1 **Raise awareness for an endangered animal.**

- Research an unusual wild animal that is endangered.
- Make posters or brochures with information about that animal.
- Share the information with your classmates.

2 **Teach others about a human-wildlife conflict.**

- Research a human-wildlife conflict where you live.
- Find out what's being done to solve this issue.
- Make a presentation to your class.

3 **Create a video interview.**

- Role-play an interview between a wild-animal expert and a journalist.
- Talk about the wild animal and the problems it faces.
- Film your interview and share it with the class.

Orphaned koalas with a carer in Queensland, Australia

Express Yourself

1 Read and listen to the story about Amy Dickman and a lion. 🎧 059

SLEEPING WITH A LION

AMY'S FIRST NIGHT IN THE WILD OF TANZANIA WAS THE SCARIEST NIGHT OF HER LIFE.

WHAT?!! MY TENT IS ON THE GROUND!?!

AMY WAS EXCITED TO BE IN AFRICA. BUT THEN SHE HEARD LIONS CALLING IN THE DARK NIGHT.

I MUST BE BRAVE!

A LION WAS WALKING AROUND AND SNIFFING HER TENT! AMY WAS AFRAID IT MIGHT ATTACK HER!

GRRR!

WHAT SHOULD I DO?!?

2 **Work in groups.** Discuss the story.

1. How did Amy's story make you feel? Explain.

2. What would you do in Amy's situation?

3. What other problems do people who work with wildlife have?

74

3 Connect ideas.
Discuss the story. In Unit 3, you learnt about what humans and animals do at night. In Unit 4, you learnt about human and animal interaction. What connection can you see between the two units?

THE LION LAY DOWN ON AMY'S ARM. IT FELL ASLEEP! AMY WAS VERY FRIGHTENED.

OH, NO! I CAN'T MOVE MY ARM!

AMY COULD FEEL THE HEAT FROM THE LION'S BODY. HER TENT BECAME VERY, VERY HOT. SHE COULD HARDLY BREATHE! SHE WAS VERY SCARED. FINALLY, SHE FELL ASLEEP, TOO.

IN THE MORNING, THE LION WAS GONE. THERE WERE PAW PRINTS ALL AROUND HER TENT.

WAS IT A DREAM?

4 YOU DECIDE Choose an activity.
1. Choose a topic:
   • the world at night
   • human and animal interaction
2. Choose a way to express yourself:
   • an oral story
   • a comic strip
   • a play
3. Present your work.

75

Unit 1

Syllables and stress

1 **Listen.** Words in English have one or more parts. These parts make up *syllables*. A syllable has a vowel sound and can also have one or more consonant sounds. Listen. Notice the numbers of syllables in these words. 🎧 116

1	2	3
▢	▢ ▢	▢ ▢ ▢
man	Ja - **pan**	Ja - pa - **nese**
street	**peo**-ple	**ci** - ti - zen
bridge	**brid**-ges	**na** - tion - al

In words with two or more syllables, one syllable is stronger than the others. The vowel in that syllable is pronounced more loudly and clearly. This is the stressed syllable. Listen again and notice the stressed syllable in the two- and three-syllable words above.

2 **Listen and repeat.** Do the word pairs have the same number of syllables? Write *Y* for *yes* or *N* for *no*. Then listen again and circle the stressed syllable. 🎧 117

1. __Y__ (Lon)don (Eng)land
2. _____ surround surrounded
3. _____ Mexico America
4. _____ travel travelled
5. _____ pavement streetlight
6. _____ explore exploration

3 **Work in pairs.** Write the words in the correct column. Then listen to the completed table to check your answers. 🎧 118

~~architecture~~	capital	design	entertainment
planned	resident	sign	unique

1 syllable	2 syllables	3 syllables	4 syllables
			architecture

Unit 2

Intonation in questions

1 **Listen.** Notice how the voice goes up or down at the end of the questions. 🎧 119

Does a pastry chef wear a uniform? ↗

Do pastry chefs work every day? ↗

How do you create beautiful desserts? ↘

Where do pastry chefs work? ↘

The voice rises at the end of questions asking for an answer of *yes* or *no*.

The voice falls at the end of questions that ask for information. These questions start with the words *who, what, when, where, why* and *how*.

2 **Listen and repeat.** Circle the correct arrow to indicate intonation for each question. 🎧 120

1. Where does he work? ↗ (↘)
2. Does she work full time? ↗ ↘
3. Who is your boss? ↗ ↘
4. Is this design yours? ↗ ↘
5. Do they like their jobs? ↗ ↘
6. When do you finish work? ↗ ↘

3 **Work in pairs.** Does the voice go up or down at the end of these questions? Draw an arrow. Then ask and answer the questions.

Do you like cake?	Yes, of course I do!

1. Do you like cake? ↗
2. When is your English lesson?
3. Do you have a busy schedule?
4. Do you do your homework every day?
5. What do you do at the weekend?

Unit 3

Present continuous: Stress of the verb *be*

1 **Listen.** Notice the pronunciation of the forms of *be*. 🎧 **121**

Akiko **isn't** sleeping.
Some animals <u>are</u> hunting.

<u>Are</u> they going to the festival?
Yes, they **are**.

<u>Is</u> she eating breakfast now?
Yes, she **is**. And we<u>'re</u> going to bed!

Be is unstressed when it's in an affirmative statement or a question.

Be is stressed when it's in a negative statement or at the end of a short answer.

2 **Listen and repeat.** Circle the stressed forms of *be*. 🎧 **122**

1. A: When is the sun coming out?
   B: It isn't coming out!
2. A: Is it raining?
   B: Yes, it is.
3. A: Which animals are sleeping now?
   B: Bears and bats.
4. A: Are the children skiing?
   B: No, they aren't.

3 **Work in pairs.** Listen and repeat the questions. Then ask and answer them with a partner. Make sure you stress *be* when necessary. 🎧 **123**

> What are you studying this week? We're studying Norway.

1. What are you studying this week?
2. Are you enjoying this weather?
3. Who are you studying with now?
4. When are you taking your next test?
5. Is your teacher smiling?

Unit 4

Can and *can't*

1 **Listen.** Notice the pronunciation of *can* and *can't*. 🎧 **124**

<u>Can</u> an alligator run?
Yes, it **can**. But you <u>can</u> run faster.

How <u>can</u> people help sea turtles?
They <u>can</u> help protect their nests.

I **can't** believe Amy's story about the lion! <u>Can</u> you?
No, I **can't**! It's amazing.

In statements and questions, *can* sounds like *kn*. The vowel *a* is weak.

In short answers and negative contractions, the vowel *a* is strong. It's pronounced fully. For example:

I **can't** see. Can you?
Yes, I **can**.

2 **Listen and repeat.** Cross out the *a* in the weak forms of *can*. 🎧 **125**

1. People <u>can</u> help animals in many ways.
2. <u>Can</u> the city build an animal crossing this year?
   No, they <u>can't</u>. They haven't got the money.
3. Elephants <u>can</u> walk under the road in Kenya.
4. Many animals <u>can't</u> safely cross roads.
5. The red crabs <u>can</u> cross the road safely now, so they <u>can't</u> be harmed anymore.

3 **Work in pairs.** Listen and repeat the questions. Then ask and answer them. 🎧 **126**

> Can you milk a cow or goat? No, I can't! Can you?

1. Can you milk a cow or goat?
2. Can you keep a baboon as a pet?
3. Where can I get a kitten?
4. What animals can we help in this country?
5. Can you make animal noises in English?

Irregular Verbs

Infinitive	Past simple	Past participle	Infinitive	Past simple	Past participle
be	were	been	leave	left	left
beat	beat	beaten	lend	lent	lent
become	became	become	let	let	let
begin	began	begun	lie (down)	lay	lain
bend	bent	bent	light	lit	lit
bet	bet	bet	lose	lost	lost
bite	bit	bitten	make	made	made
bleed	bled	bled	mean	meant	meant
blow	blew	blown	meet	met	met
break	broke	broken	overcome	overcame	overcome
bring	brought	brought	pay	paid	paid
build	built	built	put	put	put
burn	burnt	burnt	quit	quit	quit
buy	bought	bought	read	read	read
carry	carried	carried	ride	rode	ridden
catch	caught	caught	ring	rang	rung
choose	chose	chosen	rise	rose	risen
come	came	come	run	ran	run
cost	cost	cost	say	said	said
cut	cut	cut	see	saw	seen
deal	dealt	dealt	sell	sold	sold
dig	dug	dug	send	sent	sent
dive	dived	dived	set	set	set
do	did	done	sew	sewed	sewn
draw	drew	drawn	shake	shook	shaken
drink	drank	drunk	shine	shone	shone
drive	drove	driven	show	showed	shown
dry	dried	dried	shrink	shrank	shrunk
eat	ate	eaten	shut	shut	shut
fall	fell	fallen	sing	sang	sung
feed	fed	fed	sink	sank	sunk
feel	felt	felt	sit	sat	sat
fight	fought	fought	sleep	slept	slept
find	found	found	slide	slid	slid
flee	fled	fled	speak	spoke	spoken
fly	flew	flown	spend	spent	spent
forbid	forbade	forbidden	spin	spun	spun
forget	forgot	forgotten	stand	stood	stood
forgive	forgave	forgiven	steal	stole	stolen
freeze	froze	frozen	stick	stuck	stuck
fry	fried	fried	sting	stung	stung
get	got	got	stink	stank	stunk
give	gave	given	strike	struck	struck
go	went	gone	swear	swore	sworn
grind	ground	ground	sweep	swept	swept
grow	grew	grown	swim	swam	swum
hang	hung	hung	swing	swung	swung
have	had	had	take	took	taken
hear	heard	heard	teach	taught	taught
hide	hid	hidden	tear	tore	torn
hit	hit	hit	tell	told	told
hold	held	held	think	thought	thought
hurt	hurt	hurt	throw	threw	thrown
keep	kept	kept	understand	understood	understood
kneel	knelt	knelt	wake	woke	woken
knit	knitted	knitted	wear	wore	worn
know	knew	known	weave	wove	woven
lay	laid	laid	win	won	won
lead	led	led	write	wrote	written

Greetings: Formal and informal

1 **Listen and read.** 🎧 140

Formal

Ben: Hello, Mr Moore. How are you?

Mr Moore: Very well, thank you. And you?

Greeting	Responding
• Hello. How are you? • Good (morning). How are you?	• Very well, thank you. And you? • Fine, thank you. Good (morning). How are you?

2 **Listen and read.** 🎧 141

Informal

Gabi: Hi, Ben. How are you doing?

Ben: I'm OK, thanks. How are you?

Greeting	Responding
• Hi! How are you? • Hello. How's it going? • Hi. How are you doing?	• I'm OK, thanks. • Hi. I'm fine, thanks. How are you? • Great, thanks. How about you? • Not bad, thanks. You?
• Hey. What's happening? • Hey there. What are you up to? • Hey. What's going on?	• Nothing much. • Nothing special. You? • Not much. How about you?

Introductions: Formal and informal

3 **Listen and read.** 🎧 **142**

Formal

Gabi: Mr Moore, I'd like to introduce you to Ben.

Mr Moore: Hello, Ben. It's a pleasure to meet you.

Making an introduction	Responding
• I'd like you to meet Ben. • I'd like to introduce you to Ben. • Please allow me to introduce Ben. He's a student at my school. • I don't think we've met. May I introduce myself? I'm Ben.	• I'm very pleased to meet you. • It's a pleasure to meet you, Ben. • Hello, Ben. I'm glad to meet you. • Hello, Ben. I'm Mr Moore. Pleased to meet you.

4 **Listen and read.** 🎧 **143**

Informal

Ben: Hi. My name is Ben. Nice to meet you.

Gabi: Hi, Ben. I'm Gabi. Very nice to meet you, too.

Making an introduction	Responding
• Hi. I'm Ben. • Hi there. My name is Ben. Nice to meet you. • Hi, Ben. This is Gabi. She's in my class. • This is Ben. He's a student in my school.	• Hi, Ben. My name is Gabi. Nice to meet you. • Hello. I'm Gabi. Very nice to meet you, too. • Hi, Gabi. Nice to meet you. • Hi, Ben. I'm Gabi. It's nice to meet you.

Asking for permission

5 **Listen and read.** 🎧 **144**

Isabella: Mum, can I go to the cinema on Friday after school?

Mum: Sure. Who are you going with? And how are you getting there?

Isabella: I'm going with Mia and Valerie. Is it OK if we walk?

Mum: I'm afraid not. But I can take you.

Asking for permission	Giving permission	Refusing permission
• Can I/we ...? • May I/we ...? (formal) • Is it OK if I/we ...? • Do you mind if I/we ...? • Would you mind if ...? • Would it be OK if ...?	• Sure. • No problem. • Of course. • Go ahead.	• I don't think so. • I'm afraid not. • I'm sorry, but no.

Expressing thanks: Formal and informal

6 **Listen and read.** 🎧 145

Formal Mr Moore: You've been very helpful. That's very thoughtful of you.

Gabi: Of course. Please don't mention it.

Expressing thanks	Responding
• Thank you. That's very kind of you. • I appreciate your help. • Thank you. That's very thoughtful. • I'm very grateful for (your help).	• It's my pleasure. • It's no trouble at all. • Of course. Please don't mention it. • It was the least I could do. • It was no problem. I'm glad to help.

7 **Listen and read.** 🎧 146

Informal Gabi: Wow! That's so nice of you. Thanks a lot.

Ben: You're welcome!

Expressing thanks	Responding
• Thanks. • Thanks a lot. • Thanks very much. • Thanks for (asking).	• You're welcome. • It's nothing! • No problem. • Sure thing. • Any time.

Taking turns

8 **Listen and read.** 🎧 147

Rika: We have to practise the dialogue on page 86. Who should go first?

Tamiko: Why don't you?

Rika: OK, sure.

Asking	Responding	Agreeing
• Who should go first? • Do you want to say the first line? • Who would like to start?	• Why don't you? • I went first the last time. • I'd like to. • Would it be OK if I went first?	• OK, sure. • All right. • Sure. Go ahead.

Asking for and giving information

9 **Listen and read.** 🎧 148

Julia:	Hey, Carlos. Could you tell me what the maths homework is?
Carlos:	As far as I know, we just need to study for the test.
Julia:	I wonder what's on it. Do you have any idea?
Carlos:	Well, I heard that it's all of Unit 10 and the first part of Unit 11.

Asking for information	Responding
• Can/Could you tell me ...?	• I heard/read that ...
• I'd like to know ...	• As far as I know, ...
• I wonder ...	• I'm not sure, but I think ...
• Do you know?	• I'd say ...
• Do you have any idea?	• I don't know.

Making a presentation

10 **Listen and read.** 🎧 149

Fatima:	Today, we're going to talk about dinosaurs.
Rana:	We'll start by describing the different groups of dinosaurs.
Fatima:	Have a look at this poster. You'll see that there are many different groups.
Rana:	Next, let's look at what dinosaurs ate.
Fatima:	As you can see, there's a lot to learn about dinosaurs. Any questions?

Beginning	Middle	End
• Today I'm/we're going to show you ...	• Take a look at ...	• As you can see, ...
• Today I'm/we're going to talk about ...	• You'll see that ...	• Any questions?
• I'll/We'll start by ...	• Next, let's look at ...	

How many ants are there for every person in the world?

a. 1,000
b. 1 million
c. 6 million

B. one million

Which city has more bicycles than people?

a. Paris
b. Tokyo
c. Amsterdam

C. Amsterdam

Papua New Guinea is a country of seven million people. How many different languages are spoken there?

a. fewer than 30
b. between 100 and 200
c. more than 800

C. more than 800

Why is the Australian town of Coober Pedy unusual?

a. Because nobody lives there.
b. Because it has three rivers.
c. Because it's completely underground.

C. Because it's completely underground.

Which country has no rivers at all?

a. Brazil
b. South Korea
c. Saudi Arabia

C. Saudi Arabia

About how many spiders are usually in one acre of green space?

a. 100
b. 50,000
c. 100,000

B. 50,000

About how many people ride the train everyday in Mumbai, India?

a. 500,000
b. 1 million
c. 6 million

C. 6 million

Which is the only African city with a subway system?

a. Nairobi
b. Cape Town
c. Cairo

C. Cairo

In Hanoi, Vietnam, a train called the 'Doorway Railway' passes through a neighbourhood. How close does it come to the houses and shops?

a. less than 1 m. (3 ft.)
b. less than 5 m. (16 ft.)
c. less than 10 m. (30 ft.)

A. less than 1 m. (3 ft.)

What type of food museum is in Rome, Italy?

a. a pasta museum
b. a chocolate museum
c. a pizza museum

A. a pasta museum

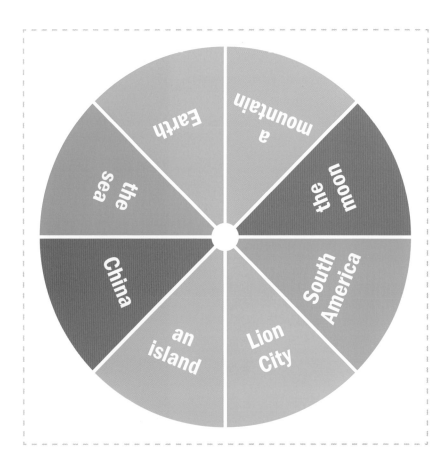

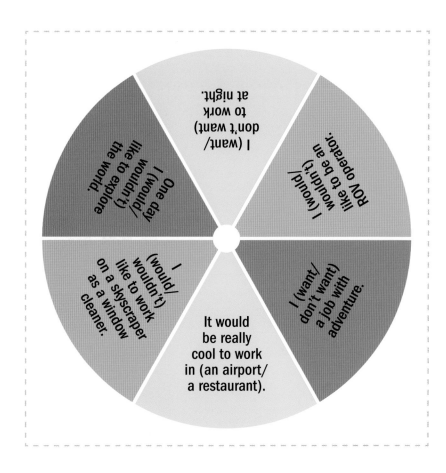

It's a **kakapo**.
Pronounced: *kah-kuh-poh*

It lives for about 60 years.

It's a **herbivore**.
- Pronounced: *hur-bih-vohr*
- Eats only plants

Tell me about this animal.

It's a **zorilla**.
Pronounced: *zuh-ril-uh*

It lives in Africa.

It's a **carnivore**.
- Pronounced: *kar-nih-vor*
- Eats mostly meat

Tell me about this animal.

It's a **bandicoot**.
Pronounced: *ban-di-koot*

It eats both plants and animals.

It's a **marsupial**.
- Pronounced: *mar-soo-pee-uhl*
- Carries its babies in a pocket or pouch

Tell me about this animal.

It's a **vinegaroon**.
Pronounced: *vin-i-guh-roon*

It's got strong claws for catching food.

It's an **arachnid**.
- Pronounced: *uh-rak-nid*
- Like a spider

Tell me about this animal.

It's a **Gila monster**.
Pronounced: *hee-luh mon-stuh*

It's nocturnal in the hot summers.

It's **venomous**.
- Pronounced: *ven-uh-muss*
- Poisonous

Tell me about this animal.

It's a **tarsier**.
Pronounced: *tahr-see-ey*

It spends most of its time in trees.

It's an unusual **mammal**.
- Pronounced: *mam-uhl*
- Feeds its babies with milk

Tell me about this animal.

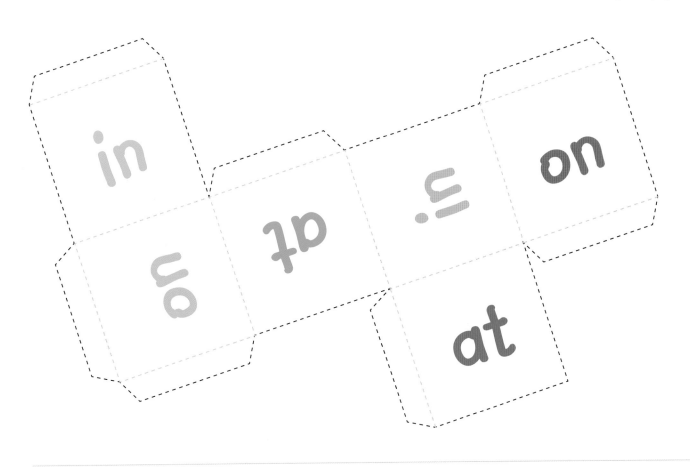

Unit 4 Cutouts Use with Activity 2 on page 70.

can	couldn't	could
could	**wild**	can't
couldn't	can	can't

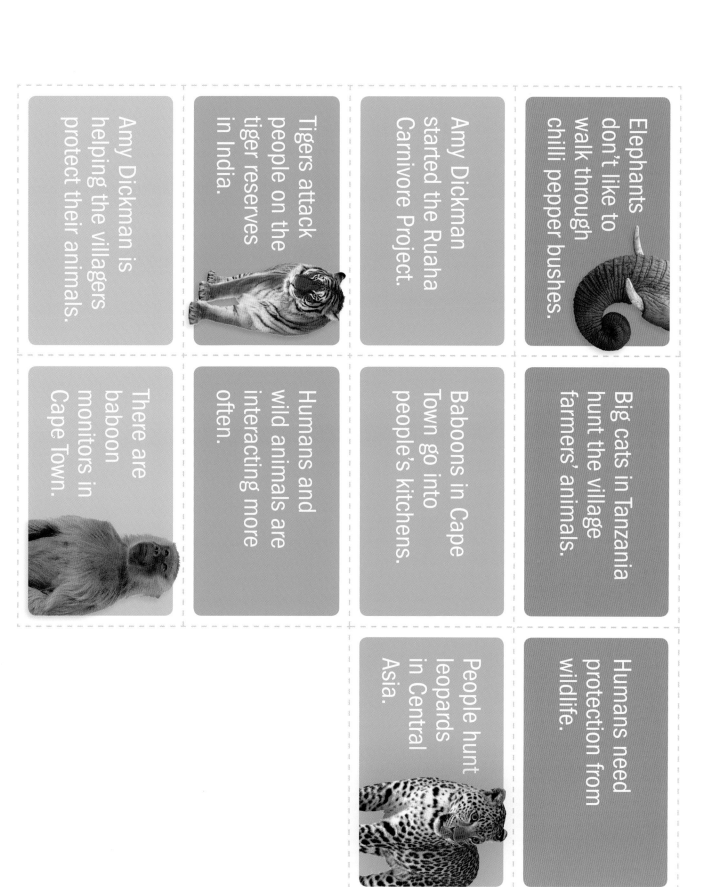

Amy Dickman is helping the villagers protect their animals.

Tigers attack people on the tiger reserves in India.

Amy Dickman started the Ruaha Carnivore Project.

Elephants don't like to walk through chilli pepper bushes.

There are baboon monitors in Cape Town.

Humans and wild animals are interacting more often.

Baboons in Cape Town go into people's kitchens.

Big cats in Tanzania hunt the village farmers' animals.

People hunt leopards in Central Asia.

Humans need protection from wildlife.

impact
WORKBOOK
1A

SERIES EDITORS
JoAnn (Jodi) Crandall
Joan Kang Shin

NATIONAL GEOGRAPHIC
L E A R N I N G

Australia · Brazil · Mexico · Singapore · United Kingdom · United States

Unit 1
Life in the City

1 **Find ten vocabulary words.** Then write the correct words to complete each sentence.

opankskyscrapersnubckbuniquenvkvufkvkfvunusualkbebfbcapitaluffjfilujlf
urbanmbdhwfulitruralubsjjshapeyeplangubbodesigninbotrtowernosid

1. People often talk about the differences between _____ life and
   _____ life. My friend is _____ because she
   lives for six months in the city and six months in the countryside.

2. I have another friend who has a very special window in his bedroom. The window is
   in the roof and is the _____ of a star. It's like sleeping under the
   stars! The _____ is _____ because he made
   it himself – nobody else has one like it!

3. Living in a _____ city is exciting. When I get a job, I
   _____ to live in Paris or Ottawa or Rome.

4. Is there a city in the world that doesn't have tall buildings or
   _____ ? Maybe, but every airport must have a communications
   _____ to help planes.

2

2 **Listen.** Write the number of the sentence that goes with each picture. 🎧 002

a.

b.

c.

d.

e.

f.

3 **Listen.** Then read and tick **T** for *True* or **F** for *False*. Rewrite the false statements to make them true. 🎧 003

	T	**F**
1. Renato is an architect.	☐	☐
2. He designs skyscrapers.	☐	☐
3. Renato's design for a city has areas only for people.	☐	☐
4. In Renato's city, cars travel above residents' heads.	☐	☐
5. Renato's design is only for older people.	☐	☐
6. Renato's city design is safe for the residents.	☐	☐
7. The bicycle tracks are high up with the cars.	☐	☐
8. Renato's city is expensive to build.	☐	☐

_____

_____

_____

_____

GRAMMAR

Present simple: General statements

Architects **design** new buildings for cities.	She **studies** the plans for the new capital.
The city's design **includes** a lot of green spaces.	The road **goes** next to an indoor park.
This tall tower **doesn't look** new.	The skyscraper **has** a garden inside.

To form the present simple, use the infinitive without *to*. *I/You/We/They* **design** *unusual buildings*. Note that with *he/she/it*, we add **-s** to the verb: *He/She* **designs** *a new skyscraper*. *It* **looks** *amazing*. To make a negative sentence, use *don't* or *doesn't*.

The spelling of some verbs changes after adding **-s** or **-es**. Add **-es** to verbs such as *cross* → *cross**es**, *wash* → *wash**es**, *watch* → *watch**es***. For verbs that end in *y*, drop the *y* and add **-ies**: *study* → *stud**ies***.

Some verbs are irregular: *go* → *go**es**, *do* → *does*, *have* → **has**.

1 **Listen.** Circle the verb you hear. Then listen again to check your answers. ⌒004

1. Capital cities **has** / **have** large public areas.

2. Children often **play** / **plays** in city parks.

3. An architect **teach** / **teaches** how to design buildings.

4. People **doesn't** / **don't** walk on this pavement.

5. Huge mountains **surround** / **surrounds** the capital city.

6. In winter the city park **closes** / **close** early.

7. She **study** / **studies** unusual architecture in Denmark.

8. The bridge **doesn't** / **don't** go to the sports centre.

2 **Write.** Fill in the blanks with the correct present simple form.

1. In Bogotá, people sometimes _____ (ride)
their bikes on the motorway.

2. Residents _____ (like) to relax
by the stream.

3. Architects _____ (not design)
skyscrapers for rural areas.

4. A new bridge _____ (cross)
the motorway.

5. People _____ (need) green spaces in capital cities.

6. Sometimes architects _____ (plan) buildings with parks on the roof.

7. In urban areas, people _____ (not enjoy) crowded pavements.

8. My village _____ (have) a water tower.

9. A major motorway _____ (connect) two big cities.

10. The stream _____ (not go) through the city.

3 **Write about a city you know.** Use some of the words in the box.

Things:	architecture	bridge	motorway	shape	pavement	skyscraper	tower
Descriptive words:	concrete	indoor	outdoor	rural	unique	unusual	urban
Verbs:	be	construct	cross	design	have	need	plan

_____

_____

_____

_____

_____

_____

4 **Draw a plan of your city.** Use a separate piece of paper. Practise talking about the details
of your plan with your classmates or teacher.

1 Listen and read. As you read, notice the separate paragraphs. Why does the writer start new paragraphs? 🎧 005

Desire* Paths

*desire   *v.* to want something
         n. the feeling of wanting something

¹Everybody has seen one, most people have walked on one, and perhaps you started a new one. We may not know the name, but these paths are called 'desire paths'. These are paths, tracks, or pavements made by people or animals walking on the grass to move quickly from one concrete pavement to another. For example, we see these paths in urban spaces where people don't use the pavements, but take a shortcut through green land, parks and gardens.

²So why do people decide to walk on the green grass and not on the pavements? Sometimes the architect's plan for urban spaces isn't the best. Residents, people like you and me, who use the outdoor areas every day, know the best and quickest way to walk from one place to another.

³The problem is that we destroy the grass when we make a desire path. Also, these new tracks get wet and dirty easily. Concrete is cleaner. We know that we need to protect our green spaces, but we also need to move from place to place quickly.

⁴Perhaps we need better designers and architects to plan our pavements and urban green spaces. They should ask local people and pay attention to what residents want.

2 **Answer the questions.** Write the number of the paragraph on the line.

_____ 1. Which paragraph gives us a definition of desire paths?

_____ 2. Which paragraph tells us about problems with desire paths?

_____ 3. Which paragraph describes the reasons for desire paths?

_____ 4. Which paragraph discusses possible solutions to the problems?

3 **Complete the diagram.** Read the text again and make notes in the boxes.

```
                                    ┌─────────────────────────────┐
                              ┌─────│ 1.                          │
                   ┌──────────┐     └─────────────────────────────┘
                   │ Reasons  │
                   └──────────┘     ┌─────────────────────────────┐
      ┌──────────────┐        └─────│ 2.                          │
      │ Desire paths │              └─────────────────────────────┘
      └──────────────┘
                   ┌──────────┐     ┌─────────────────────────────┐
                   │ Problems │─────│ 1.                          │
                   └──────────┘     └─────────────────────────────┘

                                    ┌─────────────────────────────┐
                              ┌─────│ 2.                          │
                                    └─────────────────────────────┘
```

4 **Think about the information from the texts in this unit.** You've read about desire paths and a plan to make London into a new type of national park. Read the sentences. Do you agree with these ideas? Tick (✓) the boxes if you agree. Write a question mark (**?**) if you're not sure. Write (**X**) if you don't agree.

1. There's a lot of green space where I live. ☐

2. We need to protect green spaces in cities. ☐

3. I use desire paths. ☐

4. Concrete pavements are important. ☐

5. I feel happier when I spend time outdoors. ☐

6. The walk to my nearest park is too long. ☐

7. Architects should ask city residents about their ideas for green spaces. ☐

8. People haven't got enough information about nature in urban areas. ☐

GRAMMAR

In and *on*: Expressing location

People walk **on** the grass and make new paths.	There aren't enough trees **in** cities.
There's a restaurant **on** top of the skyscraper.	We need more green spaces **in** urban areas.
I walk my dog **on** the pavement.	I like to relax **in** the park.

We use *in* and *on* to say where something is. Use *in* to give the idea that things are inside something or in an area; for example, in buildings, cities and countries. *People live **in** skyscrapers. There are many beaches **in** Rio de Janeiro. Rio de Janeiro is **in** Brazil. Brazil is a country **in** South America.*

Use *on* to say that something is on the surface or on top of something else. We also use *on* with streets and roads. *They live **on** an island. Their house is **on** Broad Street. They often walk **on** the beach.*

---

1 Circle the correct preposition.

1. Cars don't go **on** / **in** pavements.

2. There are a lot of skyscrapers **in** / **on** big cities.

3. The Statue of Liberty is **on** / **in** an island.

4. You can find lot of green areas **in** / **on** the countryside.

5. Moscow is **in** / **on** Russia.

6. The Taj Mahal is **on** / **in** India.

7. The most popular Internet café is **on** / **in** Main Street.

8. The architect lives **in** / **on** Los Angeles.

9. Many residents of Rio de Janeiro like to relax **on** / **in** the beach.

10. There's a new restaurant **on** / **in** top of the building.

2 Listen. Draw a dot *in* or *on* each box according to the sentence you hear. 🎧 006

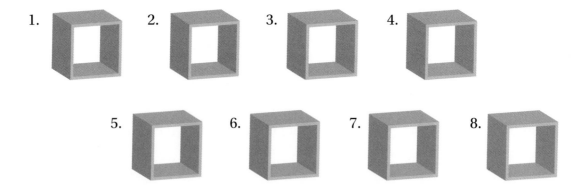

3 **Write.** Marta is in her first year at college. This is an e-mail to her younger brother. Read and fill in the blanks with *in* or *on*.

Hi Seba,

How are you? I'm fine now after two days (1) _____ my new room at college. It's really cool here. Everybody can find me easily because my name is (2) _____ the door!

I don't know the town very well yet, but my building is (3) _____ Main Street, so everything is close. I see that there's a new park near my building. Guess what? It has a skateboard track (4) _____ the middle! So bring your skateboard when you come. I think you can fit it (5) _____ your bag, can't you? Here's a photo of the park.

I'm thinking of joining a club that does something called 'Parkour'. Have you heard of it? They also call it 'urban free running' – running (6) _____ cities. Look it up on the Internet. There are some amazing videos!

Say hi to Mum and Dad, and see if you can visit me soon.

Bye for now!

Marta

---

4 **Think about the design of the neighbourhood where you live.** Write at least six sentences using *in* and *on* and the words from the box. Practise talking about your neighbourhood with your classmates or teacher.

| bridge | motorway | park | river | shopping centre | pavement | skyscraper |

I live in a skyscraper in Hong Kong.

_____

_____

_____

_____

WRITING

When we want to tell someone about a person, a place or a thing, we often use descriptive words. Words such as *dirty*, *busy* and *wet* are adjectives that go with nouns to paint a better picture in our mind. Notice how these descriptive words create different pictures in our mind.
- *Alexis skates on the **dirty** pavement.*
- *Alexis skates on the **wet** pavement.*
- *Alexis skates on the **busy** pavement.*

1 Organise.

1. Your topic is a place that needs changing. Think of a place you know that has a problem. Maybe it's very small, too dry or wet, or maybe there's a lot of rubbish there.

   In the first column, list three things you don't like about the place. Then, in the second column, think of how you can change each thing. Use descriptive words.

A place I don't like	My changes
school playground – broken bench	new, wooden bench

   Read your two lists and add more descriptive adjectives. Use a dictionary to help.

2. Plan your writing. You need an opening statement that describes the place and what the problem is. This will be your topic sentence. It helps the readers understand your idea. Write your topic sentence here:

   _____

   Next, you'll need a paragraph describing what the problem is, and a paragraph about what the place looks like after the change. Remember to use descriptive words to create a picture in your readers' minds.

2 Write.

1. Go to page 21 in your book. Re-read the model text and the descriptive words.
2. Write your first draft. Check for organisation, content, punctuation, capitalisation and spelling.
3. Write your final draft. Share it with your teacher and classmates.

Now I can ...

· **talk about cities and different types of life in the city.**

Write two sentences about urban life.

_____

_____

Write two sentences about green spaces in cities.

_____

_____

· **use the present simple to talk about general statements.**

Write four sentences using the present simple form of any of the verbs from the box. Two of your sentences should be negative.

| construct | design | explore | find | grow | live | need | pay | plan | use | walk |

_____

_____

_____

· **use _in_ and _on_ to express location.**

Write four sentences about a place you know. Use _in_ and _on_.

_____

_____

_____

· **write a description of a place in my neighbourhood.**

Use four or more descriptive words to write about a real place.

_____

_____

_____

YOU DECIDE **Choose an activity.** Go to page 90.

Unit 2
Amazing Jobs

1 **Draw.** Complete the maze by connecting all the words.

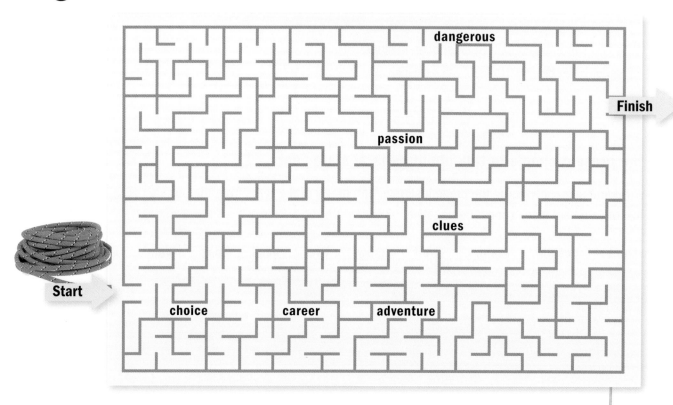

2 **Write.** Complete the sentences with the words from Activity 1.

1. She loves to cook something new every day. She has
   a _____ for cooking.

2. Guillermo has been an underwater archaeologist for many years.
   That's his _____ .

3. Would you like to work in an office or in an underwater cave?
   For me that's an easy _____ !

4. We had an amazing _____ in India! Every day we did something
   different. What a great place!

5. Divers take risks in difficult places. Their job can be _____ .

6. We had no _____ to help us find the ancient city ruins.

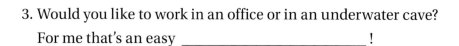

3 **Write.** Read each sentence and write the profession it describes.

archaeologist	researcher

1. This person usually **works** in an **office**. _____researcher_____

2. This person usually doesn't **work** outdoors. _____

3. This worker **considers** what is true or false and writes a report. _____

4. This person **studies** history and sometimes finds lost objects. _____

5. This worker **trains** with a team for many weeks. _____

6. This person **works** alone at a computer most of the time. _____

7. Sometimes, this person's **profession** can be **dangerous**. _____

4 **Listen.** Match each speaker to a job from the box. Write the job on the line. 🎧 007

archaeologist	diver	office worker	researcher	ROV operator

1. _____   3. _____   5. _____

2. _____   4. _____

5 **Write.** Which profession in Activity 4 is your favourite? Least favourite? Complete the sentences with your own ideas.

1. A/an _____ is my favourite of these jobs because

_____ .

2. A/an _____ is my least favourite of these jobs because

_____ .

3. I'm not sure about the job of _____ because

_____ .

GRAMMAR

Present simple questions and answers: Talking about routines

Does a water slide tester **travel** to different countries?	**Yes**, he **does**. / **No**, he **doesn't**.
Do water slide testers **get** any money?	**Yes**, they **do**. / **No**, they **don't**.
Do you **know** when a water slide isn't good?	**Yes**, I **do**. Sometimes the water **doesn't go** on some parts of the slide, or the design is not perfect, so I **stop** in the middle.
Where do water slide testers **work**?	We **work** in places such as hotels, theme parks and cruise ships.

To form questions in the present simple, use **do**/**does** and the verb (infinitive without *to*). A short answer to these questions starts with **Yes** or **No**, and we repeat **do**/**does** or **doesn't**/**don't** but not the verb. **Does** *an underwater explorer* **have** *a dangerous job?* **Yes**, *he* **does**. Sometimes, we give additional information. **Do** *you* **like** *your office?* **No**, *I* **don't**. *It's too small.*

When we look for specific information, we start the questions with questions words (*where, what, when, why* and so on). **Where do** *researchers* **work?** *They* **work** *in an office.*

1 **Read and match the questions with the answers.**
Write the letter on the line.

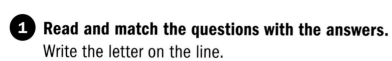

_____ 1. Does this man like his job?

_____ 2. Do people really do this job?

_____ 3. How much money does he earn?

_____ 4. Why do designers need to test slides?

_____ 5. Does he need special physical training?

a. about $30,000 a year

b. Yes, he does! He enjoys it a lot.

c. No, he doesn't. He just needs to be fit.

d. Yes, they do!

e. because water slides have to be safe and fun

2 **Listen.** Then complete the short answers. 🎧008

1. Yes, _____ I do _____ .

2. Yes, _____ .

3. No, _____ .

4. Yes, _____ .

5. No, _____ .

6. Yes, _____ .

14

3 Write. Use the words to ask questions.

1. he / speak / many languages   _____

2. you / have / accidents   _____

3. when / you / usually / work   _____

4. he / need / interview   _____

5. where / you / apply for / job   _____

6. what / he / like / about his job   _____

4 Write. Think about these unusual jobs. Imagine the answers to the questions.

1. What does a pet food tester do?

_____

_____

2. What does a dog surfing instructor do?

_____

_____

3. What does a golf ball diver do?

_____

_____

5 Choose one unusual job from this unit. Imagine you have an interview for that career. Ask and answer two questions.

Question: *What do underwater archaeologists do?* _____

Answer: *They study objects and places from the past, under water!* _____

Question 1: _____

Answer: _____

Question 2: _____

Answer: _____

Unlucky Days at Work

[1] When you choose an unusual career, like I did, you don't expect everything to be easy. I'm an underwater archaeologist, and things can go wrong. That's normal. Sometimes an advisor says that we might find bones in a cave, for example, but we arrive and it's empty. That tells me nobody lived there. So now we ask – why didn't anybody live in that cave? In this way we create new research and change a bad situation into something positive.

[2] When we explore an underwater cave, we work hard. We get up early, check our equipment, and drive for many hours. Then we get out and walk, carrying our heavy ropes and diving equipment. Like most people, we have to follow a schedule carefully. We can't spend too many hours diving.

[3] One time we got our measurements wrong. I went down into a cave on a 50-metre rope to check the cave. When I got near the bottom, the rope wasn't long enough. And then I saw that there was almost no water in the cave! I looked very funny with all my expensive diving equipment in a cave with no water! Anyway, underwater archaeology is my passion, and it's better than commuting to an office.

1. Give an example from paragraph 1 of a problem that the author had.

_____

2. How are underwater archaeologists like many people? Give two examples.

_____

3. What is one problem the author describes in paragraph 3?

_____

2 **Read the text again.** Complete the table for paragraph 1.

Paragraph 1	
Topic Sentence	
Supporting Details	
Concluding Sentence	

3 **Think about the information in this unit.** You've read about a photographer, a space scientist and an underwater archaeologist. If you agree, tick (✔) the sentence. If you don't agree, change the sentence so that it's true for you.

1. I want to be a professional photographer who works in the Himalayas.

   I don't want to be a professional photographer in the Himalayas. OR

   I want to be a professional photographer in the Caribbean.

2. Space science costs too much money. We don't need to learn about other planets.

3. Diving in a cave is probably the coolest job in the world.

4. Taking risks for your career is a bad idea.

5. Learning about the past helps us plan our future.

6. Explorers are important because we need to know more about our planet.

GRAMMAR

Possessives: Showing ownership

The **camera's** lens is broken.	**My** camera isn't working.
Thomas's dad is a photographer.	Is **his** mum a photographer, too?
NASA's new space telescope takes great pictures.	**Its** name is Hubble.
The **children's / boys'** password is new.	**Their** new password is 'adventure'.

To show that something belongs to a person or thing, we use these words: *my, your, his, her, its, our, their.*

We can also show possession by adding **'s** to a singular noun or to plural nouns that don't end in **s**: The **diver's** *job is interesting.* **Women's** *passion for diving isn't unusual.*

Add only an apostrophe (**'**) to plural nouns that end in **s**: *photographers' cameras.* Add **'s** to words that end in **s**: *Mr* **Dickens's** *house.*

1 **Listen for the possessives.** Circle the word you hear. 🎧 **010**

1. **Jupiter's / Jupiter** moon might have water.

2. The **doctors' / doctor** plane is like a flying hospital.

3. Are these **your / yours** oxygen tanks?

4. The **photographer's / photographer** camera is expensive.

5. All three **researcher / researchers'** data needs to be in one report.

6. The bicycle has lost **its / his** wheel.

7. Please order three **children / children's** meals.

2 **Write the possessive form for each noun.**

1. researcher ____researcher's____

2. women _____

3. bicycle _____

4. advisors _____

5. office _____

6. Dickens _____

7. puppies _____

8. house _____

3 **Complete the sentences.** Use the correct words from the box.

my	your	his	her	its	our	their

1. Would you like to borrow __my__ dictionary?

2. Oh no, _____ flight is late. We'll miss the connection in Madrid.

3. Excuse me, you dropped _____ ticket.

4. The divers carry _____ oxygen tanks.

5. Dr Emily Park has to change _____ schedule this week.

6. His laptop isn't working now, so he has to recharge _____ battery.

7. Tony loves _____ work. He's an underwater photographer.

4 **Listen.** Then read and tick **T** for *True* and **F** for *False*. Rewrite any false sentences to make them true. 🎧 **011**

	T	F
1. Judy's job is to explore mountains.	☐	☐
2. Judy finds cool places in Dublin where animals also live.	☐	☐
3. Street art can change an ugly urban space into a more positive environment.	☐	☐
4. Animals need green spaces in cities.	☐	☐
5. A lot of young people in Dublin go to parks.	☐	☐
6. Judy wants young people to have fun and also experience nature.	☐	☐

WRITING

When we write good descriptive paragraphs, we want our readers to understand our ideas clearly. So, each paragraph needs a topic sentence, some details, and a concluding sentence.

> **steeplejack** –*n.* a person who climbs tall buildings to clean, paint or repair them

1 Organise.

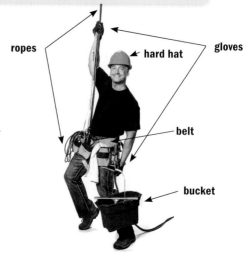

ropes · hard hat · gloves · belt · bucket

1. Your task is to write a description of someone's daily routine for an unusual profession. Look through the unit for ideas on unusual jobs or do some research on the Internet. For example, you can write about the steeplejack in the photo.

2. Plan your writing. Your paragraph needs a title and should start with a topic sentence that describes the unusual job. Then, write a few sentences about the daily routine of the person who has this unusual job. Finally, you will need a concluding sentence.

   Use the table to help you plan and list the important details of your paragraph. Think about details such as where the person works, what kind of equipment he or she needs to do the job, and what he or she does from day to day.

Title	
Topic Sentence	
Supporting Details	
Concluding Sentence	

2 Write.

1. Go to page 37 in your book. Re-read the model text and the writing prompt.
2. Write your first draft. Check for organisation, punctuation, capitalisation and spelling.
3. Check your final draft. Share it with your teacher and classmates.

Now I can ...

· **talk about unusual careers.**

Describe one of these unusual careers.

golf ball diver

_____

_____

_____

_____

pet food tester

· **use the present simple to ask and answer questions about routines.**

Complete the questions and answers with *do* or *does,* and a verb.

My uncle is a fortune cookie writer.

_____ he work every day? Yes, he _____ . / No, he _____ .

_____ you get cookies from him? Yes, I _____ . / No, I _____ .

Where _____ he _____ (work)? He _____ at home.

· **use possessives to show ownership.**

Change the nouns to possessives.

1. (Kenji) ___Kenji's___ advisor is a scientist. ___His___ advisor is a scientist.

2. (the dog) _____ food is very tasty. _____ food is very tasty.

3. (the men) _____ restaurant is underwater. _____ restaurant is underwater.

· **write a description of someone's daily routine.**

Title: _____

Topic sentence: _____

Details: _____

Conclusion: _____

YOU DECIDE **Choose an activity.** Go to page 91.

Units 1–2 Review

1 **Read.** Choose the word that best completes the sentences.

1. Tammy's brothers and sisters don't like snakes, but she does.
   Her mother says that she's _____ in her family.
   (a.) unique   b. similar   c. normal

2. Tim goes to bed at 6 a.m. and wakes up at lunchtime. He works most nights.
   He's _____ because most people work during the day.
   a. unusual   b. common   c. normal

3. Ivan asks the photographer some questions. He's _____ her for his blog.
   a. researching   b. interviewing   c. considering

4. There are lots of parks and outdoor spaces in my city. I like living in
   a(n) _____ area.
   a. rural   b. urban   c. countryside

5. I love history, so I know what profession I want to study in college. I want to
   be an _____ .
   a. architect   b. animal researcher   c. archaeologist

6. Katerina climbs towers and skyscrapers in her work. She _____ every day.
   a. takes risks   b. applies for   c. constructs

2 **Listen.** Match each teenager to a career he or she might like. Write the number on the line. 🎧 **012**

_____ a. Steeplejack – travel the country; clean, repair tall buildings

_____ b. Dog walker – outdoor spaces and parks; take dogs for walks

_____ c. Personal trainer – sports centre; help people keep fit, learn sports

_____ d. Underwater photographer – seas around the world; taking photos

_____ e. Researcher – home; collect information, interview, write reports

3 **Read.** Decide which answer (**a**, **b**, **c**, or **d**) best fits each blank space.

A Twenty-first Century Place to Live

My home is in Yangon, the old capital of Myanmar. Yangon (1) _____ city centre is changing fast; (2) _____ old buildings are being replaced by new skyscrapers. People walk on new concrete pavements. The city (3) _____ modern architecture is amazing. There are three new motorways and tall bridges over the river.

Many years ago (4) _____ family bought an apartment on Strand Road, next to the river. We could see boats from every room. Now (5) _____ kitchen only has a view of a new skyscraper. When we sit in our living room, we can see (6) _____ favourite cinema.

1.	a. 's	b. s'	c. its	d. his
2.	a. his	b. 's	c. their	d. its
3.	a. his	b. its	c. 's	d. s'
4.	a. my	b. his	c. 's	d. her
5.	a. our	b. their	c. its	d. s'
6.	a. your	b. s'	c. our	d. its

4 **Read the sentences.** Circle the correct word.

1. The motorway **don't** / **doesn't** cross the river.

2. **Do** / **Does** children play in the park?

3. Why **don't** / **doesn't** you like working in an office?

4. Maya and her daughter **plans** / **plan** a visit to the water tower.

5. **Does** / **Do** we have any clues about the unusual symbols on that wall?

6. Before Coco can go to live **in** / **on** the jungle, she must learn how to climb.

7. Commuting to the city centre is more tiring **in** / **on** a bicycle.

8. My cousin's profession is unusual. She tests pet food **in** / **on** a scientist's laboratory!

9. Architects design our pavements but they don't think about the people who walk **in** / **on** them.

10. Her brother's friend works **in** / **on** Saudi Arabia as a photographer.

Unit 3
Secrets of the Dark

1 **Read.** Decide whether each sentence describes picture A or B. Write *A* or *B*.

A

B

_____ 1. The boy is very active.

_____ 2. The boy is going to sleep.

_____ 3. It's after sunset.

_____ 4. It's daylight.

_____ 5. The streetlight is lit up.

_____ 6. The streetlight isn't lit up.

_____ 7. It's dark outside.

_____ 8. It's after sunrise.

2 **Listen.** Then circle the best answers. 🎧 **013**

1. Ella walks to school in **darkness** / **daylight**.

2. The students see the **sunrise** / **sunset**.

3. The playground is **lit up** / **not lit up**.

4. When Ella walks home from school, cars drive with **headlights on** / **headlights off**.

5. People in Stockholm **go to sleep** / **are active** when it's dark early.

3 **Read.** Then match the sentence halves about daylight hours in Stockholm.
Write the letters.

In Stockholm, Sweden, there are 18 hours of daylight during the month of June. However, in December, there are only five hours. This causes some health problems. People need the sun's vitamin D for healthy bones and skin. So the residents add extra vitamin D to their winter diet by eating more yoghurt and drinking extra milk. Also, they usually take two holidays a year to enjoy the sun.

There are other problems, too. People feel sad, lose energy, and go out to festivals less often. In the city centre, tall buildings block the sunlight from reaching the pavements, so sometimes offices and homes get less than 5 hours of light a day. However, when it snows, the city looks brighter because streetlights and cars' headlights light up the snow.

_____ 1. In the city centre, tall buildings

_____ 2. Eating more milk products

_____ 3. Some people feel unhappy

_____ 4. Although Stockholm has very few hours of sunlight in the winter,

_____ 5. One good thing is that when it snows

a. helps people be healthy in the winter months.

b. it has fewer hours of darkness in the summer.

c. the city appears lighter because of the streetlights shining on the snow.

d. when they don't have enough daylight.

e. block the sun, so it's dark.

4 **Write.** Look at the picture and write sentences.
Use vocabulary words from the word box.

| active | darkness | streetlights | sunset |

1. _____

2. _____

3. _____

4. _____

GRAMMAR

Present continuous: Saying what is happening now

Non-action verbs	Action verbs
We **understand** your idea.	She**'s wearing** snow boots.
She **doesn't think** it's expensive.	I**'m ice-skating** on the lake.
They **stay** at their grandmother's house in the summer.	You**'re learning** about time zones.
You **look** healthy.	They**'re making** a green glowing light.

Some verbs describe actions: *learn, skate, sing, grow, climb*. We can use the *be + –ing* form with these verbs. *Now we* **are learning***. I'm **skating***. They***'re singing***.

Other verbs don't describe actions. We use them to describe situations, feelings and ideas: *be, live, believe, understand, have, hear, want*. We don't often use the *be + –ing* form with these verbs.

Some non-action verbs can become action verbs with a change in meaning; for example: *think, have*. *I* **think** *this sunset is beautiful. I* **am thinking** *of the sunset I saw yesterday.*

1 **Choose the correct verb to complete each sentence.** Think about if the sentence describes something happening now (*action verb*) or something that is always true (*non-action verb*).

1. She **is wearing** / **wears** a hat and gloves when it is cold at night.

2. He **believes** / **is believing** there's life on Mars.

3. Animals that glow in the dark **include** / **are including** fireflies and jellyfish.

4. David Gruber often **surfs** / **is surfing** when he goes on holiday.

5. Scientists **are learning** / **learn** that more underwater creatures glow in the dark.

6. Kids **love** / **are loving** unusual animals.

7. I'm busy right now. I **am working** / **work** on my report.

2 **Listen.** Circle **A** for *Action* and **NA** for *Non-action*. 🎧 **014**

1. **A** **NA**   3. **A** **NA**   5. **A** **NA**   7. **A** **NA**   9. **A** **NA**
2. **A** **NA**   4. **A** **NA**   6. **A** **NA**   8. **A** **NA**   10. **A** **NA**

3 **Write.** Put each word under **Day** (sun) or **Night** (moon). Add more words using your own ideas. Then write five sentences using the words from the lists.

| awake   car headlights   dark   darkness   daylight   go to sleep   streetlight   sunset |

Day ☀	Night ☾

1. _____

2. _____

3. _____

4. _____

5. _____

4 **Finish these sentences.** Use vocabulary from this unit. Don't forget to use negatives.

1. During the day, a DJ *goes to sleep because he works at night* .

2. We use streetlights so _____ .

3. In Stockholm, people _____ .

4. At sunset tonight, they _____ .

5. People in many countries use fireworks when _____ .

6. Today, we _____ .

27

1 **Listen and read.** As you read, underline the words in bold type from pages 44–45 of your student's book. The first word is done for you. 🎧 **015**

Festival of Lights

Diwali, the Hindu <u>festival</u> of lights, is a fascinating tradition in India. It celebrates the victory of light over darkness and right over wrong. There are some differences in how people observe this festival around the country. In the north, people celebrate the story of a great king's return to his kingdom. In the south, people celebrate it as the day that they fought a great battle. In the west of India, the festival remembers that light returns to Earth, and in the east, people pray for strength. During the festival, there are glowing lights everywhere. People light traditional oil lamps and fireworks.

There are five days of *Diwali*. On the first day, people clean their homes and go shopping for clothes, gold and kitchen utensils. On the second day, people have a bath before sunrise and then decorate their homes with clay lamps. They also create patterns on the floor using colourful powder or sand. The third day is the most important day of the festival. On that day, families share amazing meals and watch fireworks all night until dawn the next day. The fourth day is the first day of the Hindu New Year. On that day, friends and relatives visit with gifts and best wishes. On the last day, brothers visit their married sisters, who welcome them with a tasty meal.

2 **Read.** Tick **T** for *True* or **F** for *False*.

	T	F
1. *Diwali* is a Buddhist festival.	☐	☐
2. Different parts of India celebrate for different reasons.	☐	☐
3. People light fireworks.	☐	☐
4. *Diwali* celebrations go on for four days.	☐	☐
5. People create patterns on the walls of their homes.	☐	☐
6. During the celebration, people visit each other.	☐	☐

3 **Write.** List the activities for the five days of *Diwali* and the reasons people celebrate it in different parts of India.

Day 1: _____

Day 2: _____

Day 3: _____

Day 4: _____

Day 5: _____

North: _____

East: _____

South: _____

West: _____

4 **Write.** How are the *Diwali* festival of lights and the Chinese Lantern Festival similar? Different? Fill in the Venn diagram.

Diwali   **Both**   **Chinese Lantern Festival**

home celebration   bright lights   street celebration

5 **Write.** Imagine you are a writer for your school website blog. Write a few sentences about a local festival you went to.

_____

_____

_____

GRAMMAR

At, *on* and *in*: Saying when things happen

Our New Year starts **on** 1st January.	There's no school **on** Thursday. It's a holiday!
Stockholm has only five hours of daylight **in** November.	**In** the evenings, my brother is less active.
During the *Diwali* festival, people have a bath **at** dawn.	The sun rises **at** 9.30 **in** the morning.

We use *on* for days of the week and for specific dates: **on** *Tuesday (morning)*, **on** *6th June*.

We use *in* with months, years, seasons and periods of time: **in** *February*, **in** *2017*, **in** *(the) winter*, **in** *the morning*, **in** *a minute*.

We use *at* with exact times and certain expressions: **at** *sunset*, **at** *lunchtime*, **at** *3.45 p.m.*

1 **Listen.** Circle *in*, *on* or *at*.  016

1. Many plants grow (**in** / **on** / **at**) night.

2. The Chinese New Year festival is usually (**in** / **on** / **at**) February.

3. My parents eat lunch (**in** / **on** / **at**)12.30 p.m.

4. DJs usually work (**in** / **on** / **at**) the weekend.

5. People have a bath (**in** / **on** / **at**) sunrise during the *Diwali* festival.

6. I was born (**in** / **on** / **at**) 2004.

7. These festivals start (**in** / **on** / **at**) the evening.

8. See you (**in** / **on** / **at**) Tuesday morning.

9. Birds are very active (**in** / **on** / **at**) dawn.

10. Don't forget his birthday! It's (**in** / **on** / **at**) 1st April, too!

2 **Read Carlos's blog.** Then answer the questions using *at*, *on* or *in*.

Day 1: Iceland's unique landscape, with its snowy mountains and frozen lakes, is a perfect place for photographers like me. It's mid-winter, and I hear that all over the country you can see the famous Northern Lights, or *Aurora Borealis*. I'm looking forward to seeing the night sky lit up with green, red, yellow and purple light. The best view is around midnight, they say. So, here I am! I checked into my hotel. My camera battery is charging, and I'm waiting for the sunset! See you tomorrow!

Gallery

1. What time of year are the Northern Lights visible?

_____

2. What time of day or night gives the best view of the Northern Lights?

_____

3. When is the photographer going outdoors to take a photograph?

_____

3 **Read Carlos's blog from Day 2.** Complete the sentences with *at*, *on* or *in*.

Incredible! I can't believe how beautiful the sky was last night. I left my hotel (1) _at_ 3.30 (2) ____ the afternoon. The sunset was soon after that, (3) ____ around 4.00. The weather here is freezing. It's 23 degrees Fahrenheit (-5 C) (4) ____ sunset. I don't like standing around outside (5) ____ winter, so I decided to go back into the hotel.

(6) ____ about 8.00 (7) ____ the evening, I put on my hat and went outside again. Perfect timing! An amazing green light glowed in the sky in front of me, with lines of purple and red. Wow! More people were outside by now, watching in silence. Click on the gallery link to see my photos. More tomorrow! Flying home (8) ____ Tuesday.

WRITING

We can talk about an event using the five senses as we describe what we see, hear, taste, smell and feel. With sensory words, our readers imagine that they are there at the event.

1 **Organise.**

1. Your task is to describe a colourful event, for example, a festival, fireworks, a sunset or watching a wood fire.

2. Plan your writing. Your paragraph should start with an introductory sentence that describes the colourful event. Use the hand below to write three or more sensory words to describe what you see, hear, taste, smell and feel. If needed, use a dictionary to help.

   Write your introductory sentence here:

   _____

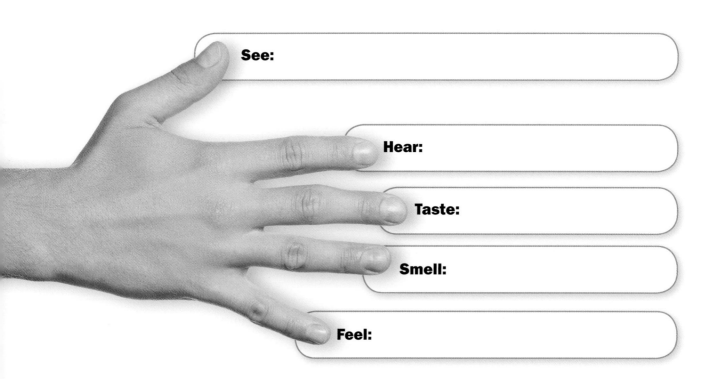

See:

Hear:

Taste:

Smell:

Feel:

3. In your paragraph, use the sensory words you listed to help you describe the colourful event. Finish your paragraph with a brief statement of why this event is special and how you feel about it.

2 **Write.**

1. Go to page 55 in your book. Re-read the model and writing prompt.

2. Write your first draft. Check for organisation, content, punctuation, capitalisation and spelling.

3. Write your final draft. Share it with your teacher and classmates.

Now I can ...

- **talk about night, darkness and nocturnal activities.**

  Choose a nocturnal animal and a light festival. Write two sentences about each.

  1. _____

  _____

  2. _____

  _____

- **use non-action and action verbs.**

  Write two sentences using action verbs and two sentences using non-action verbs.

believe	feel	glow	shine	understand	watch

  1. _____

  2. _____

  3. _____

  4. _____

- **use *at, on* and *in* to say when things happen.**

  Write sentences using the following information.

  1. morning / watch / sunrise _____

  2. weekend/ ride a bike / park _____

  3. observe / animal / night _____

- **write a description of an event using adjectives and the five senses.**

  Use sensory words to describe your experience at a fireworks show.

  _____

  _____

  _____

YOU DECIDE Choose an activity. Go to page 92.

Unit 4
Living Together

1 **Read the clues.** Then complete the words.

1. ____ i ____ ____ l ____ ____ ____   Animals that live in their natural setting

2. ____ ____ ____ f ____ ____ ____ t ____   Fights, disagreements

3. ____ ____ ____ a ____ ____ ____ ____ r   To go away so we can't see something

4. m ____ ____ ____ r ____ ____ ____   To injure, hurt or be unkind to someone or something

5. ____ c ____ e ____ ____   A way in

6. ____ a ____ ____ t ____ ____   Animals' natural homes

2 **Read.** Complete each sentence with a word from **Activity 1**.

1. At sunset, wild animals come close to the tent, and then they _____.

2. People who don't take care of their pets _____ them.

3. Amy Dickman studies _____ between wild animals and humans.

4. We had _____ to the mountain area to observe the wild cats.

5. The snow leopard's _____ is in cold, mountainous areas.

6. There's a special relationship between people and _____ .

3 **Listen.** Then tick **T** for *True* or **F** for *False*. Rewrite the false sentences to make them true. 🎧 **017**

		T	**F**
1. The programme was about animals.		☐	☐
2. He thinks that dogs are wild.		☐	☐
3. She thinks that Siamese crocodiles aren't very clever.		☐	☐
4. The crocodiles' habitat doesn't have any water.		☐	☐
5. We can't live without water.		☐	☐
6. Little animals catch crocodiles.		☐	☐

_____

_____

_____

4 **Read.** Number the sentences in order.

_____ We want to educate the villagers so that they can learn safe ways to live with the wildcats.

_____ To help them, we need to find $2,000 to spend on saving the wildcats in my grandfather's village.

_____ It's called 'Save the Wildcats' because we want to help the survival of these animals in Peru.

_____ Good morning, everyone. I want to explain our project to you.

_____ Please give money or your time to help Peru's amazing wildlife live together with local people. Thank you for listening!

_____ People living in the mountains frighten the wildcats away when they use the land for their farms.

Peruvian wildcat

5 **Write.** Complete the notes about the project in Activity 4.

1. In Peru, some villagers are _____.

2. The busy farms _____.

3. At the moment, people don't want to help the cats because_____.

4. This project can help people _____.

5. I think I should _____.

GRAMMAR

Modals: Describing obligation and advice

Necessary	We **must help** endangered animals survive. We **have to allow** sea turtles to lay their eggs on our beaches. A conservationist **has to work** in difficult places.
Not necessary	An animal conservationist **doesn't have to be** male. They can be male or female.
Recommended (should/shouldn't)	We **should learn** more about the behaviour of unpopular animals, such as rats. People **shouldn't be** afraid of Antiguan racer snakes.

To say that something is necessary, we use the words **have to** and **must**. They have almost the same meaning, but **must** is stronger; there is no other choice. In negative statements, **don't have to** shows that something isn't necessary. To give advice, we use **should**. Use **should** to say it's a good idea, and **shouldn't** to say it's not a good idea.

---

1 **Write.** Use *must, have/has to, don't/doesn't have to,* or *should/shouldn't* according to the clues given in brackets.

1. Sea turtles are endangered. We _____ protect them. (necessary)

2. People _____ have picnics on beaches where there are sea turtle eggs. (not a good idea)

3. We _____ use plastic bags when we go shopping. (not necessary)

4. We _____ recycle paper. (necessary)

5. People _____ be very careful around mother cats who defend their kittens. (a good idea)

6. You _____ use the car every day. (not necessary)

7. You _____ interact with injured animals. (not a good idea)

8. Animals and people _____ drink water to survive. (necessary)

2 **Listen.** Is the idea *necessary*, *not necessary*, or *recommended*?
Tick the correct answer. 🎧 **018**

	Necessary	Not necessary	Recommended
1.	☐	☐	☐
2.	☐	☐	☐
3.	☐	☐	☐
4.	☐	☐	☐
5.	☐	☐	☐
6.	☐	☐	☐
7.	☐	☐	☐
8.	☐	☐	☐

3 **Write.** Look at the pictures. Use the clues and *must*, *has/have to*, *doesn't/don't have to*, or *should/shouldn't* in your sentences.

1. snake handler / gloves

_____

2. lion / circus

_____

3. bird of prey / fish

_____

4. turtle / plastic bags

_____

Stop the boat party –
Lamma Island's sea turtles are in danger!

When you think of Hong Kong, you probably don't think of **wildlife**, do you? But one of Hong Kong's islands, Lamma Island, is also home to endangered green sea turtles. Between June and October, they come to the island's Sham Wan beach to lay their eggs.

Special nature police must keep people away from the turtles. At nesting time, you shouldn't go near the beach. If the police see you, you have to pay a fine, which can be a lot of money. However, the police aren't always there to protect the area. The biggest problem is human **behaviour**. Boat parties play loud music, and tourists go swimming and have picnics, which **frightens** the turtles away. Scientists and conservationist groups say we **need** a bigger restricted* area to help the turtles **survive**.

Experts agree that green sea turtles in Hong Kong are in danger. The turtles are **disappearing**. One scientist said, 'When a turtle is **afraid of** going onto the beach, it has to lay its eggs underwater, where they die.' In 2006, there were 14 records of nesting turtles in Sham Wan beach but only two after that, and not a single turtle has been seen since 2012. Another expert said that the number of turtles should increase in the future because now people are working on creating a better **relationship** with the turtles.

***restricted** adj. with limits, closed-off

2 **Read the text again.** Find four problems (causes) that contribute to a result (effect) for the green sea turtles.

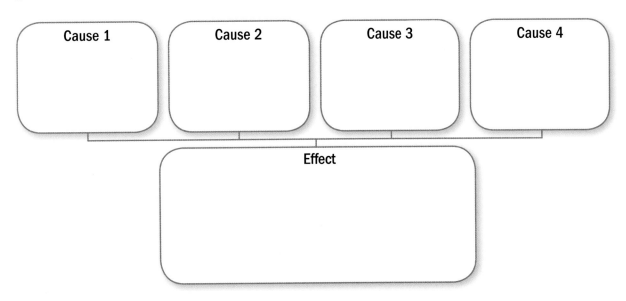

3 **Summarise the text.** Tell someone about the Hong Kong green sea turtles. Write sentences about the problems, the results and a possible solution.

    1. One problem for the turtles is that _____.

    2. Another problem for the turtles is _____.

    3. A third problem for the turtles is _____.

    4. Conservationists think _____.

    5. One solution is _____.

4 **Write.** Think about the information from the texts in this unit. You have read about different problems between humans and animals. Complete the list of advice.

At home: We _____.

At the beach: People _____.

In the mountains: Villagers _____.

GRAMMAR

Modals: Describing ability in present and past

Crocodiles **can sleep** with one eye open.	At that time, turtles **could lay** their eggs on the beaches.
Most domestic animals **can't survive** in the wild.	Conservation groups **couldn't rescue** all the birds.
Why **can't** we **interact** with wildlife easily in a city?	The injured deer **couldn't avoid** the predators.

We use *can/can't* to talk about ability in the present. We use *could/couldn't* to talk about ability in the past.

1 **Listen.** Circle the word you hear. 🎧**020**

1. The baby panda **can / can't** see people.

2. They **could / couldn't** understand animals before.

3. Trained dogs **can / can't** sniff for chemicals.

4. They **can / can't** drive to the injured snow leopard.

5. They **could / couldn't** save all the birds.

6. We **can / can't** avoid using plastic bags.

7. The turtles **could / couldn't** lay their eggs.

2 **Read.** Underline the phrases with *can*, *can't*, *could* or *couldn't*. Then circle the correct word to complete the sentence.

The Survival of the Antiguan Racer Snake

The Antiguan racer is probably the world's least known snake. It's not dangerous and it can't kill you. However, these snakes are slowly disappearing from Bird Island, a small island off the coast of Antigua. How can we save these racers?

Conservationist Jenny Daltry studies the snakes, so we can now understand the Antiguan racers' habitat and behaviour. During her five-year project, they have removed the racers' biggest predators, black rats, from the island. Now the rats can't prey on the snakes' eggs. However, the snakes can still die because of hurricanes or bad weather conditions, other predators and tourists.

Sadly, there's also another problem. Bird Island is so small that only about 100 racer snakes could survive there. Jenny's team hopes that they can introduce racers to other nearby islands. They have already saved the Antiguan racer; we can be sure that, without this project, this snake would disappear.

You can read about Jenny's project in an article on the Internet.

Because of this project, more racer snakes **can** / **can't** survive on Bird Island.

3 **Read the article again.** Complete these sentences using *can*, *can't*, *could* or *couldn't*.

1. The Antiguan racer snakes _____.

2. Black rats _____.

3. Jenny and her team _____.

4. The five-year project _____.

5. Hurricanes, predators and tourists _____.

6. Researchers hope that _____.

7. This project means that now people _____.

8. You _____ on the Internet.

After you write, you need to read your work and check it. Ask yourself some questions: Is my writing organised? Are the ideas clear? Circle any spelling and grammar mistakes. Finally, rewrite your work and proofread it for any last changes.

1 Organise.

1. Your topic is a relationship between a person and an animal. Think of a relationship you know, have read about, or seen in a film. How would you describe the relationship? Make a list of your ideas in the table.

Person	Animal

2. Plan your writing. You'll need an introductory paragraph with a topic sentence. Your topic sentence will state the relationship between the person and the animal. Write your topic sentence here:

_____

Next, you'll need a paragraph to describe the relationship and how the person and animal interact. Explain the situation with a few details.

Remember to finish your paragraph with a brief statement of why this relationship is special.

2 Write.

1. Go to page 37 in your book. Re-read the model and writing prompt.

2. Write your first draft. Check for organisation, content, punctuation, capitalisation and spelling.

3. Write your final draft. Share it with your teacher and classmates.

Now I can ...

· **talk about interactions between animals and humans.**

☐ Yes, I can!
☐ I think I can.
☐ I need more practice.

Describe the relationship of the man and the baby elephant.
Write two or three sentences.

_____

_____

_____

· **use modals to describe obligation and advice.**

☐ Yes, I can!
☐ I think I can.
☐ I need more practice.

Complete the sentences according to the clues. Use *must, has/have to,*
doesn't/don't have to or *should/shouldn't.*

1. I _____ help this injured animal, so it can survive.
   (very necessary)

2. Animals have feelings, too. You _____ mistreat them. (advice)

3. We _____ keep the seas free of plastic bags. (necessary)

· **use modals to describe ability in the present and past.**

☐ Yes, I can!
☐ I think I can.
☐ I need more practice.

Complete the sentences with *can/could* or *can't/couldn't.*

1. A mountain lion _____ climb over a 12-foot wall.

2. When it was born, the baby panda's eyes were closed. It _____ see.

3. Yesterday, they _____ rescue some sea turtles.

· **write a description of a special relationship between an animal
and a human.**

☐ Yes, I can!
☐ I think I can.
☐ I need more practice.

Describe a situation in which an animal interacts with a human.

_____

_____

_____

YOUDECIDE Choose an activity. Go to page 93.

Units 3–4 Review

1 **Read.** Then choose the correct words.

A
Please don't call me today.
I'm not feeling very well and
(1) **I'm staying / I stay** in bed.
Call me (2) **on/ at** about 10.00
tomorrow morning. I (2) **want /
am wanting** to check our science
project before class (3) **on / at**
Monday.

B
After our meeting today, I had another idea.
I can't (1) **go to sleep / asleep** without telling
you. I think we can ask teachers to talk to
students about how important it is to (2)
interact / rescue with wildlife and learn about
the animals' behavior and habitat. We can
write a letter (3) **in / at** the morning to local
schools. What do you think?

C
Are you (1) **observe / observing** wildlife? Don't forget to take photographs of the birds, mice, rabbits and
insects around your home (2) **on / in** the weekend! Get
up early both days, (3) **on / at** sunrise. Bring your
photos to Monday's club meeting (4) **at /on** 1 p.m.

2 **Listen.** Then choose the best answer. 🎧 **021**

1. Cars _____ .

   a. stop to rescue salamanders
   b. kill salamanders in the darkness
   c. with headlights help salamanders

2. The speakers agree that _____ .

   a. salamanders are very clever
   b. salamanders are afraid of cars
   c. salamanders should move faster

3. Snakes _____ .

   a. hunt salamanders
   b. don't hunt salamanders
   c. eat insects

3 **Read.** Choose the best answer for each blank.

A conservation magazine reports that we must try to (1) _____ the destruction of our planet. When people cut down trees to construct new buildings, they are destroying animals' (2) _____ . Forests are homes to thousands of (3) _____ animals. Now these animals (4) _____ find new places to live. Some animals go into towns and villages because they can't (5) _____ for food in the forests. It (6) _____ dangerous in North Canada, for example. While people are (7) _____ , wild bears have easy access to waste food in rubbish bins. Our relationship with animals (8) _____ change if we want to share our planet.

1. **a.** avoid   **b.** keep   **c.** not
2. **a.** horizon   **b.** time zones   **c.** habitats
3. **a.** tame   **b.** wild   **c.** clever
4. **a.** have to   **b.** need   **c.** should
5. **a.** observe   **b.** defend   **c.** hunt
6. **a.** is becoming   **b.** are becoming   **c.** should becoming
7. **a.** asleep   **b.** awake   **c.** injured
8. **a.** couldn't   **b.** shouldn't   **c.** must

4 **Read the sentences.** Use the words in the box to complete the second sentence so that the meaning is the same as the first sentence. Use no more than one word for each blank.

at	couldn't	mistreat	observe	predator	relationship	sunrise	sunset

1. While people are asleep, wild bears hunt for food in North Canada. Wild bears sniff around the rubbish bins in North Canada _____*at*_____ night.

2. When it's early morning in Europe, it's 12.30 p.m. in India. When I see the _____ here in Spain, my friend in India is finishing her lunch!

3. I think the sky is more beautiful when the sun goes down. I believe _____ is more beautiful.

4. The world of insects fascinates me. I love to _____ ants, spiders and tiny animals.

5. People interact with domestic animals. Pets, such as cats and dogs, are easy to have a _____ with.

6. Snakes eat mice and salamanders. Salamanders and mice have the same _____ – snakes.

7. Reports say that aquatic parks treat dolphins and whales very well. I hope that aquatic parks don't _____ their sea creatures.

8. Yesterday the rats were not able to sniff any of the landmines. The rats _____ find any landmines yesterday.

☐ **1** Use words from the list to talk about life in one of your favourite places.

motorway	indoor	land	outdoor
park	rural	surrounded by	unique
unusual	urban		

☐ **2** Use present simple verbs you know and the words in the list to make positive and negative statements about a place you know.

architecture	concrete	construct	design
land	live	plan	

_____

_____

_____

_____

☐ **3** Complete each sentence using your own ideas. Use *in* or *on* in each sentence.

This skyscraper is unusual because it has

_____

That tower is unique. It

_____

That park is a new design. It

_____

☐ **4** **Work in pairs.** Interview an architect.

- Research an architect.
- Prepare three questions about the buildings she or he designs. Make notes about the answers to your questions.
- Assign the roles of interviewer and architect.
- Practise the interview.
- Act out the interview in class, or use a phone or tablet to make a video.

☐ **5** **Write.** Think of a place that makes you happy. Describe it.

- To plan your writing, follow the steps on page 10 of your workbook.
- Share your writing with your teacher and classmates.

☐ **6** **Write.** You see this poster on a local notice board.

Design Competition

Local residents, now you can help to plan your capital city! This is a unique chance to give architects your ideas about urban spaces and the architecture you're surrounded by. Do you have any unusual ideas for bridges, towers, skyscrapers or pavements?

Send an e-mail to a friend describing your ideas. Write at least 100 words.

1 Connect words from the two word boxes to talk about careers.

| advisor | archaeologist | photographer |
| researcher | scientist | |

| adventure | dangerous | explore |
| office | passion | schedule |

2 Use present simple verbs to ask and answer questions. Use words from the list.

| apply for | commute | consider | create |
| explore | study | take risks | train |

3 Complete each sentence with a possessive.

We left _____ plans on the table. Please bring them here.

The photographer can't find _____ camera. Is it in your office?

Two researchers need to apply for _____ jobs again. Let's interview them next week.

Look at that building! _____ shape is very unusual.

I love _____ job. I explore underwater caves.

4 **Work in pairs.** Have a conversation about work. Repeat the activity in class, or make a video on your phone or tablet.

Tell your partner about someone you know who has an interesting job and the work they do. Include:

- the name of the job
- where he or she works
- what he or she does
- special skills
- any special study or training.

5 **Write.** Think of an unusual career you know something about. Describe it. Where does it take place? What's hard about it. What's fun?

- To plan your writing, follow the steps on page 20 of your workbook.
- Share your writing with your teacher and classmates.

6 **Write.** Your friend sends you a message.

Dangerous jobs?

Hi,

This week my school project is about difficult careers. I think unusual – and even dangerous – jobs are interesting, don't you? Do you know anything about dangerous or unusual jobs?

Reply and describe your ideas. Write at least 100 words.

☐ **1** Describe things that happen during the day and at night. Use words from the list.

darkness	fascinate	glow
go to sleep	light up	nocturnal
observe	streetlight	

☐ **2** Use action and non-action verbs to describe the things in the word box.

Example: *At dawn we see the sunrise. The sun is rising now, and I'm watching it!*

dawn	daylight	festival
headlights	horizon	streetlights
sunrise	sunset	time zones

☐ **3** You received a text message from a cousin who just moved to your neighbourhood. Answer the questions using *at, on* or *in*.

Hi! Sorry to text again, but I forgot to ask you some questions.

When are you home?

What time do you go to sleep?

In the mornings, are you usually awake when it's still dark?

When is the best time to call you? Evenings? Saturday mornings?

Also, I want to take photos of my new house and the view. When is the sunset tonight?

See you at school!

☐ **4** **Work in pairs.** You want to walk to your friend's house after dark. Your parents don't like the idea. Role-play the dialogue.

- Choose roles (yourself, your mum or dad).
- Think about the road, the pavement, the streetlights, the car headlights and the time.
- Practise the dialogue. Change roles, and practise the dialogue again
- Assign final roles.
- Act out the dialogue in class, or use a phone or tablet to make a video.

☐ **5** **Write.** Think of an event that usually happens at night. Use sensory words to describe the event.

- To plan your writing, follow the steps on page 32 of your workbook.
- Share your writing with your teacher and classmates.

☐ **6** **Write.** Your teacher asks you to write a story. This is the title of the story.

My Five Senses Saved Me!

Write your story. Write at least 160 words.

1 Spin a paperclip to choose words from the circle. Use the words you land on to make sentences about wildlife.

behaviour

defend

prey

feelings

predator

habitat

2 Give advice to young people about living together with wildlife. Use words from the list and *must, should/shouldn't* and *have/has to* or *don't/doesn't have to*.

afraid of	avoid	frighten
hunt	learn	mistreat
rescue	survive	

3 Think of a predator you know about. What is its prey? Use *can, can't, could* and *couldn't* to describe its behaviour.

4 **Work in pairs.** Plan an interview with an animal conservationist.

- Research a conservationist who works with animals.
- List several things about his or her work that interest you.
- Prepare three questions about his or her work. Make notes about the answers to your questions.
- Choose roles and practise the interview with a partner.
- Act out the conversation in class, or use a smartphone or tablet to make a video.

5 **Write.** Think about someone you know. Then choose an unusual animal. Imagine a scene in which they interact. The scene can be realistic, or it can be a fantasy.

- To plan your writing, follow the steps on page 42 of your workbook.
- Share your writing with your teacher and classmates.

6 **Write.** Read the advertisement. Then write an e-mail.

Photo Story

Are you a good photographer? We need amazing photos that show relationships between people and unusual animals.

Write an e-mail to a person who interacts with an unusual animal. Describe your ideas for a photo story. Write at least 100 words.